P9-DDS-037

WALLINGFORD PUBLIC LIBRARY
200 North Main St.
Wallingford, CT 06492

WITHDRAWN

HIP-HOP STARS

RUSSELL SIMMONS

HIP-HOP STARS

Beastie Boys
Sean Combs
Missy Elliott
Eminem
Jay-Z
LL Cool J
Queen Latifah
Run-DMC
Tupac Shakur
Russell Simmons

HIP-HOP STARS

RUSSELL SIMMONS

Cookie Lommel

WALLINGFORD PUBLIC LIBRARY
200 North Main St.
Wallingford, CT 06492

CHELSEA HOUSE
PUBLISHERS
An imprint of Infobase Publishing

YA B
SIMMONS
LO

RUSSELL SIMMONS

Copyright © 2007 by Infobase Publishing

All rights reserved. No part of this book may be reproduced or utilized in any form or by any means, electronic or mechanical, including photocopying, recording, or by any information storage or retrieval systems, without permission in writing from the publisher. For information contact:

Chelsea House
An imprint of Infobase Publishing
132 West 31st Street
New York, NY 10001

Library of Congress Cataloging-in-Publication Data

Lommel, Cookie.
 Russell Simmons / Cookie Lommel.
     p. cm. — (Hip-hop stars)
 Includes bibliographical references and index.
 ISBN-13: 978-0-7910-9467-9 (hardcover)
 ISBN-10: 0-7910-9467-7 (hardcover)
 1. Simmons, Russell—Juvenile literature.   2. Sound recording executives
and producers—United States—Biography—Juvenile literature.   3. Def Jam
Recordings. I. Title. II. Series.
 ML3930.S545L66 2007
 782.421649092—dc22
 [B]
                                   2007001463

Chelsea House books are available at special discounts when purchased in bulk quantities for businesses, associations, institutions, or sales promotions. Please call our Special Sales Department in New York at (212) 967-8800 or (800) 322-8755.

You can find Chelsea House on the World Wide Web at http://www.chelseahouse.com
Text design by Erik Lindstrom
Cover design by Ben Peterson

Printed in the United States of America
Bang NMSG 10 9 8 7 6 5 4 3 2 1

This book is printed on acid-free paper.

All links and Web addresses were checked and verified to be correct at the time of publication. Because of the dynamic nature of the Web, some addresses and links may have changed since publication and may no longer be valid.

CONTENTS

Hip-Hop: A Brief History

Like the air we breathe, hip-hop seems to be everywhere. The lifestyle that many thought would be a passing fad has, three decades later, grown to become a permanent part of world culture. Hip-hop artists have become some of today's heroes, replacing the comic book worship of decades past and joining athletes and movie stars as the people kids dream of being. Names like 50 Cent, P. Diddy, Russell Simmons, Jay-Z, Foxy Brown, Snoop Dogg, and Flavor Flav now ring as familiar as Elvis, Babe Ruth, Marilyn Monroe, and Charlie Chaplin.

While the general public knows many of the names, videos, and songs branded by the big companies that make them popular, it's also important to know the holy trinity, the founding fathers of hip-hop: Kool DJ Herc, Grandmaster Flash, and

Afrika Bambaataa. All are deejays who played and presented the records that rappers and dancers delighted themselves upon. Bambaataa single-handedly stopped the gang wars in the 1970s with the themes of peace, unity, love, and having fun.

Hip-hop is simply a term for a form of artistic creativity that was spawned in New York City—more precisely, the Bronx—in the early to mid-1970s. Amidst the urban decay in the areas where black and Hispanic people dwelled, economic, educational, and environmental resources were depleted. Jobs and businesses were all but moved away. Living conditions were of a lower standard than the rest of the city and country. Last but not least, art and sports programs in the schools were the first to be cut for the sake of lowering budgets; thus, music classes, teaching the subject's history and techniques, were all but lost.

From these ashes, like a phoenix, rose an art form. Through the love of technology and records found in family collections or even those tossed out on the street, the deejay emerged. Different from the ones heard on the radio, these folk were innovating a style that was popular on the island of Jamaica. Two turntables kept the music continuous, with the occasional voice on top of the records. This was the very humble beginning of rap music.

Rap music is actually two distinct words: rap and music. "Rap" is the vocal application that is used on top of the music. On a vocal spectrum, it is between talking and singing and is one of the few alternatives for vocalizing to emerge in the past 50 years. It's important to know that inventors and artists are side by side in the importance of music's development. Let's remember that inventor Thomas A. Edison created the first recording, with "Mary Had a Little Lamb" in 1878, most likely in New Jersey, the same state where the first rap recording— Sugarhill Gang's "Rapper's Delight"— was made more than 100 years later, in 1979.

It's hard to separate the importance of history, science, language arts, and education when discussing music. Because of the social silencing of black people in the United States from slavery in the 1600s to civil rights in the 1960s, much sentiment, dialogue, and soul is wrapped within the cultural expression of music. In eighteenth-century New Orleans, slaves gathered on Sundays in Congo Square to socialize and play music. Within this captivity many dialects, customs, and styles combined with instrumentation, vocals, and rhythm to form a musical signal or code of preservation. These are the foundations of jazz and the blues. Likewise, it's impossible to separate hip-hop and rap music from the creativity of the past. Look within the expression and words of black music and you'll get a reflection of history itself. The four creative elements of hip-hop—emceeing (the art of vocalization); deejaying (the musician-like manipulation of records); break dancing (the body expression of the music); and graffiti (the drawn graphic expression of the culture)—have been intertwined in the community before and since slavery.

However, just because these expressions were introduced by the black–Hispanic underclass, doesn't mean that others cannot create or appreciate hip-hop. Hip-hop is a cultural language used best to unite the human family all around the world. To peep the global explosion, one need not search far. Starting just north of the U.S. border, Canadian hip-hop has featured indigenous rappers who are infusing different language and dialect flows into their work, from Alaskan Eskimo to French flowing cats from Montreal and the rest of the Quebec's provincial region. Few know that France for many years has been the second largest hip-hop nation, measured not just by high sales numbers, but also by a very political philosophy. Hip-hop has been alive and present since the mid-1980s in Japan and other Asian countries. Australia has been a hotbed in welcoming world rap acts, and it has also created its own vibrant hip-hop scene, with the reminder of its government's takeover of indigenous people reflected in every rapper's flow and rhyme. As a rhythm of the people, the continents of Africa and South America (especially Ghana, Senegal, and South Africa, Brazil, Surinam, and Argentina) have long mixed traditional homage into the new beats and rhyme of this millennium.

Hip-hop has been used to help Brazilian kids learn English when school systems failed to bridge the difficult language gap of Portuguese and patois to American English. It has entertained and enlightened youth, and has engaged political discussion in society, continuing the tradition of the African griots (storytellers) and folk singers.

For the past 25 years, hip-hop has been bought, sold, followed, loved, hated, praised, and blamed. History has shown that other cultural music forms in the United States have been just as misunderstood and held under public scrutiny. The history of the people who originated the art form can be found in the music itself. The timeline of recorded rap music spans more than a quarter century, and that is history in itself.

Presidents, kings, queens, fame, famine, infamy, from the great wall of China to the Berlin wall, food, drugs, cars, hate, and love have been rhymed and scratched. This gives plenty reason for social study. And I don't know what can be more fun than learning the history of something so relevant to young minds and souls as music.

The Father of Hip-Hop

Do you listen to Def Jam recordings? Do you wear Phat Farm clothes? Chances are, you or someone you know does, and the person responsible for Def Jam and Phat Farm as well as a host of other familiar products, Russell Simmons, has a message for you: "I want young people to look inside and not to listen too much to other people—listen to yourself." Simmons told participants at a youth conference that he wants students everywhere to look inside themselves for answers, not let others think for them. Most of all, he commands his millions of listeners worldwide, "Make choices yourself as individuals that will make a difference in the world."

Russell Simmons is legendary as the hip-hop pioneer who took urban music mainstream, but he has a serious message.

11

Russell Simmons is a pioneer of hip-hop culture. Cofounder of Def Jam Recordings and creator of the urban fashion line Phat Farm, Russell Simmons is responsible for bringing hip-hop to a mainstream audience.

He's using his status to drive hip-hop culture in a new direction: giving back to the community. Now rap, once the refuge of gangsters as well as genuine artists, must answer Simmons' fiercely posed challenge, "What else?"

Simmons is fond of asking that question. He is personally driven to achieve, always looking for the next goal to meet. Russell was once a poor street kid from Queens, New York. Now he is a rap mogul with a business empire that includes everything from music to fashion, jewelry, and beverages. He produced a pre-paid Visa debit card for people who have been denied bank accounts due to low income or bad credit. Simmons's deeply held belief is that financial literacy should be an important part of everybody's education.

Financial literacy means understanding how money works. Successful rappers who overcome poverty know something that kids locked in poverty don't: how to make whatever money they have work for them. Whatever decisions a young person makes today affect the opportunities they will have tomorrow. Simmons' 2006 "Get Your Money Right Tour" was devoted to the idea that the hip-hop generation must know the "basics of banking, repairing and understanding credit scores, wealth management, vehicle financing, and home ownership, particularly if they have to start with a very slim budget," Russell explained to Vibe.com.

Simmons views rap as a force for social justice unparalleled by anything in our history. In Simmons' vision of the future, rap is a vehicle for promoting the financial literacy that can help to raise countless kids from poverty and ignorance. Rap has the ear of the young. They are listening to Simmons, music and fashion entrepreneur. And, he is rising to the challenge of speaking for them.

THE UNITED NATIONS

In fact, when Russell Simmons speaks, even the United Nations listens. In May 2006, Simmons addressed his favorite audience, kids, at the UN's Global Classrooms: New York City Model UN

Conference, sponsored by the United Nations Association of the United States (UNA-USA) and financial powerhouse Merrill Lynch.

As the keynote speaker, Simmons broached the all-important theme recognized by the UN as crucial to the development of children worldwide: The importance of being knowledgeable about the world is central to success, and knowledge comes from communicating with others. In fact, UNA-USA President William H. Luers stated, "The world will be a better place when young people like you can communicate that the world has to work together." Simmons agreed: "I want to inspire you to . . . look inside and make decisions to uplift everyone and everything around you. Be the light around you." Luers told *Vibe* magazine that Simmons was the "logical" choice to be the keynote speaker because of his "personal philanthropic efforts," which are impressive.

"I want to contribute more to earth than I take away from it," Simmons explained to Vibe.com reporter Shayla Byrd. His statements emphasize his determination to give back to the struggling urban neighborhoods like those of his youth.

For example, strengthening relations between individuals and between communities infuses the work of Simmons' own organization, The Rush Philanthropic Arts Foundation. In 2002, he also joined the board of The Foundation For Ethnic Understanding, an organization devoted to furthering positive communication between different ethnicities. He now serves as chairman. In June 2005, Simmons and rapper Jay-Z launched the Ethnic Foundation's International Anti-Semitism and Anti-Racism Public Service Announcement Campaign. Simmons, credited by many for giving African-American music culture a national voice, aims to combat discrimination between African-American and Jewish communities by bringing young people together, in line with the expressed goal of the UNA Global Classroom event that promoted understanding between cultures.

The foundation's programs are very hands on, reflecting the active leadership style of Simmons and his diverse and qualified personnel. Students retraced the journey of the civil rights movement during the summer, meeting with leaders

THE RUSH PHILANTHROPIC ARTS FOUNDATION

The Rush Philanthropic Arts Foundation provides disadvantaged children access to the arts and "provides exhibition opportunities for underrepresented artists and artists of color." Rush and Simmons have awarded more than a million dollars in grants to Impact Repertory Theatre, Youth Speaks NY, The Drawing Center, Free Arts for Abused Children, Studio in a School, Children's Museum of Manhattan, Art State, P.E.N.C.I.L., and the Los Angeles Educational Partnership. The Rush Arts Gallery and Resource Center further helps the community.

Simmons also lends support to other nonprofit, charitable groups such as Hale House, designed to help children and families by offering 24-hour infant care, primarily for those suffering from AIDS and drug addiction; Harbour House, which also provides services for those in need; the Fresh Air Fund; and various AIDS organizations. The Foundation for Ethnic Understanding, another of Simmons's social action groups, coordinates the dialogue between groups such as the NAACP and the Jewish Anti-Defamation League.

Simmons, once identified as merely another bad-boy hip-hopper from the streets of New York, works tirelessly to create a hip-hop empowered world of social change. Simmons's ability to "keep it real" and accessible allows him to connect in an unforgettable way with everyone from the kid on the street to the icons of American business.

from the African-American and Jewish communities such as Simmons, visiting major civil rights landmarks in the South as well as Jewish memorials, and attending religious services at synagogues, mosques, and Baptist churches.

THE FOUNDATION FOR ETHNIC UNDERSTANDING

On June 16, 2005, foundation President Rabbi Marc Schneier spoke to a group of students from the nonprofit organization Cultural Leadership. This program, founded by Karen Kalish, who previously had launched Operation Understanding to create positive communications between members of different ethnic communities, fights discrimination between African-American and Jewish groups by addressing and educating youths about race relations and by promoting public dialogue. Rabbi Schneier discussed Simmons's promotion of such accountability, as well as the history of African-American and Jewish relations, in the newspaper *Ha'aretz*. He also discussed his own book, *Shared Dreams*. "It was a pleasure meeting with these students and talking to them," Schneier said. "This is what the foundation is about—promoting dialogue—and there is no better way to start than with our youth," stated Schneier.

He may have been expressing Simmons's own credo. In 2001, Simmons cofounded, with Dr. Benjamin Chavis Muhammad, the Hip-Hop Summit Action Network (HSAN). HSAN is dedicated to harnessing the cultural relevance of hip-hop music to serve as a catalyst for education advocacy and other societal concerns fundamental to the well-being of at-risk youths throughout the United States. HSAN is the largest nonprofit, national coalition of hip-hop artists, entertainment industry leaders, education advocates, civil rights proponents, and youth leaders united in the belief that hip-hop can be an influential agent for positive social change and must be responsibly and actively utilized to fight the war on poverty and injustice.

In 2004, in the midst of the heated U.S. presidential campaign between Sen. John Kerry and President George W. Bush,

In the photograph above, Short Dawg *(left)*, Rev Run *(center)*, and Russell Simmons *(right)* attend the third annual Hip-Hop Summit on Financial Empowerment in Houston, Texas. Simmons cofounded the Hip-Hop Summit Action Network (HSAN) in 2001 with the hopes of empowering youth by using hip-hop music and culture. The 2007 Financial Empowerment Tour had a panel of experts teaching young people about personal finances and how to build wealth.

the Hip-Hop Summit Action Network witnessed the fruits of 18 months of inspiring and mobilizing young people to go to the polls: long lines of young voters. In fact, according to data from The Center for Information and Research on Civic Learning and Engagement (CIRCLE), 47 percent of 18 to 24 year-olds turned out, up from 36 percent in 2000.

To mark the fifth anniversary of HSAN, cofounders Chairman Russell Simmons and President and CEO Dr. Benjamin Chavis Muhammad ring The NASDAQ Stock Market Opening Bell on June 14, 2006. The Hip-Hop Summit Action Network is the largest nonprofit, national coalition of hip-hop artists and entertainment executives who believe that hip-hop can be used as a catalyst for positive social change.

Since April 2003, the Hip-Hop Team Vote Youth Voter Initiative, launched in Detroit with rappers Eminem and Nas, has registered young people at 26 summits across the country. Its Philadelphia Summit in August 2003 was the first summit to directly link youth voter registration to a celebration of hip-hop culture.

Besides registering young people to vote in conjunction with a variety of grassroots partners in each of its summit cities, HSAN also sponsored a Get Out the Vote bus tour, which brought such major names as Ludacris, Jay-Z, P. Diddy, the G Unit, and MC Lyte to cities on its route. In addition, audiences were treated to Jim Jones and the Diplomats, Ying Yang Twins, Freeway, Layzie Bone, Loon, Styllion, Miss Jade, Mr. Cheeks, Luther Campbell, and Coo Coo Cal. In Miami, superstar recording artists Missy Elliot and Tweet came out and encouraged young people to vote. In Philadelphia, Simmons and his brother, Reverend Run of Run-DMC, descended on the Famous Deli with Mayor John Street. They addressed 4,000 volunteers at the Wachovia Center and visited the Strawberry Mansion polling site, where crowds of young people had gathered to vote.

Since its star-studded inception, the HSAN has been involved in a number of blockbuster projects to promote social change. Every year, HSAN gives out awards to those individuals, groups, and entities that promote its agenda of public dialogue and social justice. In November 2005, for example, the HSAN awards were held in New York City. The awards honored such diverse recipients as Chrysler Financial, Destiny's Child, Jermaine Dupri, and Nelly for "the positive work they have put into utilizing the power of hip-hop for positive social change."

Another HSAN focus is the necessity for financial literacy, particularly for the poor, who are often overlooked in financial education, although they are most in need of its empowering ability. In 2006, following the tremendous success and positive feedback of the 2005 "Get Your Money Right" financial empowerment national tour, HSAN geared up to launch the next "Get Your Money Right" tour in Michigan at Wayne State University with sponsors Chrysler Financial and Anheuser-Busch. The press asked, "Can Russell Simmons make debt consolidation hot?"

Simmons has stated that financial empowerment is the mission of HSAN because "economics is the last leg of the civil rights movement." He explained to the *St. Louis Post-Dispatch*

During the 2004 presidential election, Russell Simmons and HSAN did their part in mobilizing young people to vote. HSAN partnered with *The Doug Banks Morning Show* with the hopes of registering 2 million voters up through the 2004 campaign and 20 million voters in the next five years. In the photograph above, Russell Simmons *(left)*, Def Jam Records President Kevin Liles *(center)*, and hip-hop artist LL Cool J *(right)* raise one finger during the launch of the "One Mind. One Vote" campaign.

that "young people get out there and make mistakes with their money, and they spend a lifetime trying to make up for it."

He also told Gail Appelson at the *St. Louis Post-Dispatch*, that teenagers identify with rappers because "their songs are about the lifestyle of those who are locked out of the American economy." The people reached by rappers include those who "don't have bank accounts, they can't rent a car, they can't get a hotel room." These same urban poor have no credit cards, or, if they do, do not know how to manage credit card debt. "The people who need the most pay the most. It's a terrible set-up. We're not educated about managing our lives."

This lack of education is HSAN's target. Simmons laments, "A lot of young people don't know their credit score or what it takes to manage a relationship with the world financially. It's simply not given enough attention." For example, a national survey of high school seniors demonstrated that although almost a third used credit cards, they did not understand the finance questions relating to their purchases. The disturbing results were released by the Jump Start Coalition for Personal Financial Literacy.

Once attacked by critics for its visual connection to an underworld of gangsters and crime, hip-hop has also been on the hot seat for promoting displays of material wealth. Simmons defends a focus of financial literacy in the face of criticism regarding the already "uber-materialistic" world. He told The Associated Press, "We do what people need. . . . The resources, underwriting change in our community, growth and economic development, those things aren't taught at all. It's just not a part of the education process, so it's important that we bring this out."

Gerrod Parchmon of Chrysler Financial, a panelist at the HSAN summit on financial literacy, defends the appropriateness of hip-hop's focus on financially educating the young. He comments that audience members pay attention to what hip-hop artists say. Such attention can make all the difference.

He echoes the president of the UNA-USA, William Luers, who explained to a group at a UN conference about the presence of Russell Simmons at the Global Classroom event. Luers said, "He's been such a major figure in building diversity, and he's someone who can relate to our students' world. Somebody like me, because of my age, experience, and background, can't connect to these kids the way he can." Aware of his ability to influence the community, Simmons has chosen to give back. His charities are the focus of "all of his spirit" and include a dizzying array of philanthropic work.

Mogul-to-Be

The key to Russell Simmons's success may very well have been his parents. "You can be whatever you want to be," Russell's mother, Evelyn, told him and his brothers. Evelyn had earned degrees in sociology and psychology from Howard University in Washington, D.C. At Howard, Evelyn met Daniel Simmons, a history major who wanted to be a teacher; both Evelyn and Daniel were "educated and quite worldly," Russell recalled in an interview with Nelson George. Evelyn had come from a tradition that emphasized initiative and achievement: Her own mother had been one of the first black nurses in her native New York.

Russell Simmons is also a New Yorker born and bred. He first greeted the world on October 4, 1957. He lived in his birthplace—Jamaica, Queens—until he was eight years old. His earliest impressions, he told George, include powerful memories of a solid, loving family. He remembers walking under Jamaica Avenue train tracks and holding hands with both parents.

He and his two brothers, Daniel Duane Simmons Jr. and Joseph Ward Simmons, grew up knowing that his parents were strong and independent in an era that was challenging for African Americans. In an interview with filmmaker Mary Mazzio of Babson College, Russell and his brothers remember that his mother didn't let racism stop her from doing things that were forbidden to blacks at that time, such as trying on clothing in department stores. "My mother was very self-confident. She knew who she was and would not let anybody, with their conceptions of African Americans, daunt her," said Daniel Simmons in the documentary *Lemonade Stories*.

THE COLLEGE-EDUCATED SIMMONS FAMILY

Their experiences were somewhat unusual at that time; the Simmons boys were to become the third generation of college-educated, home-owning African Americans. Their father was a teacher and then an attendance supervisor in Queens. Their mother was a recreation director for the New York City Department of Parks. Both parents were politically aware. Russell told George about walking a picket line with his father to protest housing and employment discrimination when he was still a boy.

His father also recited from William Shakespeare and wrote poetry. Later, he wrote some of the rhymes for Run-DMC, on songs such as "Thirty Days" and "You're Blind." He did not, however, encourage his sons to become artists. Russell's mother told him, "Do whatever you want. You can be an artist. You can be an entrepreneur." His father wanted him to go to college instead. It might have seemed natural that Russell and his brothers would follow in his parents' educated, hardworking footsteps

Russell Simmons *(right)* grew up in a tight-knit family in Hollis, Queens. His younger brother Joey *(left)* followed him into the music business and created the highly-influential group Run-DMC. Together, they were pioneers of rap music as we know it today. Now known as Rev Run, Joey has a reality show on MTV that is produced by Russell.

right away, but the changing times created different opportunities for the Simmons brothers.

In 1965, the Simmons family moved to Hollis, a middle-class, diverse residential area in Queens. In the racially charged atmosphere of the 1960s, as African Americans moved in, many whites left in an expression of bigotry known as "white flight." The neat two-story homes, with driveways and little yards, were stressed by the influx of drug dealers who took the place of the fleeing businesses. Joseph Simmons remembered, "Ghetto Street hardcore reality was only two blocks away. On the corner of Hollis . . . we weren't really allowed to go there after 6 o'clock. It got kinda bad."

MOVING IN THE WRONG DIRECTION

Russell got caught up in the market of his neighborhood, as did his brother Daniel, who explained regretfully in the documentary *Lemonade Stories,* "The biggest heartache I gave my mother was probably drugs. They were the scourge of my community."

Russell concurred. He discussed the role models of his neighborhood, "The only entrepreneurs we knew were the numbers guys and the drug dealers." It was not so surprising, then, that he began to make bad choices—choices that he now regrets and discusses with teenagers who are tempted to follow in the path that took such a toll on his own family. Russell recalled selling marijuana on a street corner and viewing himself for the first time as an entrepreneur. At age 17, however, his brother Daniel, who always admired Russell, was introduced to heroin. At first, peer pressure blinded Daniel to reality. He commented, "Every one of my friends was using heroine intravenously. . . . We didn't see ourselves as junkies, although we had to shoot heroin every day."

There were grim consequences. Daniel Simmons Jr. ended up in jail, which he said opened his eyes. Russell got arrested, disappointing his mother. His father was furious. Russell had pot in his pocket, and his father told him he was "trying to break in jail."

His parents were a rock at this turning point. His mother gave him money to promote his club shows. Russell remembers this act of support daily: "I speak to kids," he told an interviewer in *Lemonade Stories,* "and one thing I can tell them that there is never a success level. There's only this kind of thing that happens in your heart. And what happened in my heart was her encouragement."

The Simmons brothers were lucky they did not meet the same fate as many of their friends in the neighborhood. Many ended up in jail or dying, several from AIDS. Later, Russell would focus a portion of his success on helping others at critical points in their lives, when they had already gotten several strikes against

REV RUN WANTS TO BE QUEENS POET LAUREATE

What is a poet laureate? It has been described as an officially-appointed poet who is acclaimed as the most excellent or most representative of a locality or group. This could well describe hip-hop pioneer Joseph "Run" Simmons of the rap group Run-DMC. In 2004, Run decided to apply to become poet laureate of the New York borough of Queens, where he was born. Rev Run helped define the rap sound—which some regard as a form of poetry.

Rev Run believes he deserves the position because Run-DMC was created in and influenced by Hollis, Queens. However, a controversy arose, because he moved to New Jersey in 2005. Though Rev Run had wide support from many people, there was also intense objection from the poetry community. Two poets from Queens argued that rap is not a form of poetry and that rappers should not be eligible for the appointment.

Rev Run included the lyrics to one of Run-DMC's songs, "Christmas in Hollis," in his application. Run-DMC were the first rappers to have a platinum-selling album, have their videos played on MTV, and appear of the cover of *Rolling Stone* maga-zine. Queens's previous poet laureate was Hal Sirowitz, who served from 2000 to 2003. Unfortunately Rev Run's bid for poet laureate of Queens was rejected.

them. His own bad choices helped teach him compassion, as his strong family ties had taught him persistence—and love.

The core of the Simmons family is undoubtedly love, fostered especially by Evelyn Simmons. Joseph said of his mother: She "had a lot of love, a lot of hugs, and she cared so much for me." Russell told *Lemonade Stories* interviewer Mary Mazzio, "I could feel her love every time I looked at her." Evelyn Simmons's lessons for success stuck with her children. After her death, Daniel Simmons, in an interview at age 49 with his siblings, was still able to say easily of Russell, "That's my little brother. I love him." The boys, as adults, continued to be close. Their love for one another, self-confidence, and strong support system got them through tough times and helped them achieve success.

Building a
New Industry

In 1977, 20-year-old Russell Simmons experienced his first full encounter with the burgeoning rap presence in New York's club scene. At the time, MCs, or the masters of ceremonies (sometimes spelled emcee), presented performers, spoke to the audience, and generally kept the show moving. They engaged in call and-response shouts to revelers and recited their own rhymes while disc jockeys or DJs spun break beats, or loops of instrumentals, taken from popular disco and funk records.

One day, Simmons walked into a club in Harlem named Charles Gallery of 125th Street. On the mic was an MC who called himself Eddie Cheeba. As his DJ, Easy G, spun the records providing the break beat, Cheeba whipped the crowd into a frenzy with his call-and-response routine to partygoers. Simmons was caught up in the charged atmosphere created by Cheeba and quickly sniffed out an opportunity to make some money. With his days of selling drugs behind him, the budding entrepreneur began planning ways to earn a living in the promotion of hip-hop.

"All the street entrepreneurship I'd learned selling herb, hawking fake cocaine and staying out of jail, I decided to put into promoting music," Russell says in his book, *Life and Def: Sex, Drugs, Money + God.*

Acknowledging his own lack of musical talent, Simmons felt the best way to take advantage of the new movement was to produce hip-hop tracks and promote MCs. Still working toward his sociology degree at the Harlem campus of City College of New York, Simmons began organizing campus rap shows and block parties while running with a crew of hip-hop promoters calling themselves "The Force."

Simmons scouted for acts; booked venues such as Charles Gallery of 125th Street, Club 371, Smalls Paradise, and Terrible Tuesdays; and marketed the shows by putting up posters and handing out fliers. Money was scarce in the early stages of his fledgling company, so he often asked the rappers at his shows to perform for a portion of the door take.

Simmons recalls being completely broke following one party that failed to turn a profit, or even one partygoer, "I remember sitting outside and my mother coming out. She gave me money . . . and it was enough to start me over again and give me another opportunity. It was a tremendous push, because it wasn't the money, it was the investment in me. It was the belief in my future."

Refusing to throw in the towel, Simmons kept on promoting and soon found himself with a roster of artists who would one day be considered the forefathers of hip-hop, including Grandmaster Flash, D.J. Hollywood, and Harlem native Curtis Walker, who would soon earn worldwide fame as rapper Kurtis Blow.

Born August 9, 1959, Blow began his hip-hop career as a break-dancer before trading in his boombox in 1976 for two turntables, used for a process called turntabling. It was around this time that Blow first met Simmons at City College of New York. Blow served as program director for the college radio

HISTORY OF RAP MUSIC

Rapping in hip-hop music can be traced back in many ways to its African roots. Centuries before the United States existed, the griots (folk poets) of West Africa were rhythmically delivering stories over drums and sparse instrumentation. Because of the time that has passed since the griots of old, the connections between rap and the African griots are widely recognized but not clear-cut. Such connections, however, have been acknowledged by rappers, modern-day "griots," spoken-word artists, mainstream news sources, and academics.

The first modern rap recording was made in 1979 by the Sugarhill Gang and was called "Rapper's Delight." In addition to rap music, the hip-hop subculture also includes other forms of expression, including break dancing, graffiti art, a unique slang vocabulary, and fashion sense.

Rap originated in the mid-1970s within the African-American community in the South Bronx area of New York City, and it was initially recorded by small, independent record labels and marketed almost exclusively to a black audience. This new style gradually attracted white musicians, a few of whom began performing it. A remake of hard-rock band Aerosmith's "Walk This Way" in 1986, with Aerosmith teaming with Run-DMC, brought hip-hop wide popular appeal. Soon after 1986, the use of sampling and unique vocal styles became widespread in popular music.

Kurtis Blow *(above)* is considered the first rap artist to achieve commercial success. Blow was the first act Russell Simmons managed, and he often allowed Joey Simmons to deejay on his gigs, under the name "Son of Kurtis Blow." Today, Blow works behind the scenes to promote hip-hop music, and he still tours on occasion.

station by day and a block party and club DJ by night under the moniker Kool DJ Kurt.

By 1977, the lure of the microphone became too strong, and Kurt decided to test his skills as a rapper. At the suggestion of Simmons, he changed his name to Kurtis Blow and quickly developed a following in rap's underground scene. Soon, the Harlem MC was performing alongside Grandmaster Flash and, for a short time, Simmons' younger brother Joseph, who dee-jayed under the nickname Son of Kurtis Blow before changing it to Run years later.

Sensing a breakout star among his stable of artists, Russell Simmons eventually became Blow's manager and quit City College of New York to pursue the new endeavor full time. With only a few credits to go before graduating with a soci-ology degree, Simmons left it all behind and founded Rush Management, after his childhood nickname. Simmons began promoting Blow around Queens as the borough's "No. 1 rap-per," who could rhyme and spin records simultaneously. With Blow emerging in 1979 as an underground superstar through-out New York, a journalist for *Billboard* magazine wrote a pro-file about the young talent, then approached Blow's manager with a major request.

Earlier that year, the rest of the world had been introduced to hip-hop via the Sugarhill Gang's smash hit "Rapper's Delight." Borrowing the track from Chic's "Good Times," the New York City-based trio—Wonder Mike, Big Bank Hank, and Master Gee—took the song to No. 36 on the U.S. pop charts and No. 4 on the U.S. R&B charts. Despite its popularity, the song, as well as the rap genre itself, were dismissed by critics as a fad.

Billboard writer Robert Ford knew better. Believing the bur-geoning genre would have staying power, he teamed with J.B. Moore to write "Christmas Rappin,'" a hip-hop song he wanted Blow to record and put out as a single. Simmons jumped at the chance. For the first time, the Hollis, Queens, native entered the studio to coproduce a record.

During this time, Simmons also had a friend and business mentor in Roger Ford, a record producer who met the budding mogul in the early 1980s on the club circuit and began consulting him with inquiries about the industry. According to the book *Black Enterprise Titans of the B.E. 100s*, Ford's biggest advice to Simmons was to find something unique about his artists that was marketable and to always have an entertainment attorney available to review contracts whenever booking a gig.

With this knowledge and copies of Blow's "Christmas Rappin' " in his hands, Simmons hit the New York streets to stir up interest in the project. He sold copies wherever he could—at clubs, during shows, at block parties, even from the trunk of his car.

Simmons's efforts gave "Christmas Rappin'" street buzz, and soon the initial trickle of attention turned into an avalanche. Ford arranged for Simmons to meet with disc jockeys at urban radio stations to get airplay and expand the audience. With the song suddenly a fixture on radio playlists, Blow's first single quickly caught fire and became a regional hit, selling more than 50,000 records.

The accomplishment, however, was not enough for Simmons. His next challenge was to get Blow signed with a major record label so that "Christmas Rappin' " could benefit from nationwide marketing and distribution. But even with "Christmas Rappin' " a hit, record labels were still leery of the new art form.

"There was interest, but no one was biting," Simmons said in *Life and Def: Sex, Drugs, Money + God*. "The industry's attitude was that 'Rapper's Delight,' despite its U.S. sales and international appeal, was an unrepeatable fluke."

THE FIRST RECORDING DEAL

PolyGram was among the labels unsure of hip-hop's longevity. When approached by Simmons and a pitch to distribute "Christmas Rappin'," the label turned him down flat. But the young promoter would not give up that easily. Simmons visited record

Whodini *(above)* was a popular rap group in the 1980s, managed by Russell Simmon's Rush Artist Management. Rush Artist Management represented many popular rap artists such as LL Cool J, Run-DMC, and the Beastie Boys, to name a few.

stores that expressed interest in the record and told them to call PolyGram if they wanted to order copies. The plan turned out to be genius. When the telephones at PolyGram began ringing nonstop for orders of Blow's record, the label took advantage of the opportunity to cash in. In joining PolyGram's Mercury Records imprint in 1980, Kurtis Blow became the first rapper ever to sign a record deal with a major label. With its major-label push, "Christmas Rappin' " became a nationwide hit, as did its follow-up, "The Breaks," which went on to become hip-hop's first certified gold record, selling at least 500,000 copies.

MY FIRST AIRPLANE TRIP

"I remember that when the record came out, it was successful in Amsterdam, and [Blow] and I got on a plane—and I had never been on a plane—and went to Amsterdam, and the record execs took us out," Simmons said in a 2002 interview with Ken Paulson of the First Amendment Center. "It was the most amazing thing that ever happened to me. I was thrilled that I was in the record business, and I was, you know, important, getting flown around, and I think that's when I was the most successful, 'cause that was an amazing transformation, just being able to travel and be part of a culture and actually be part of it growing within an industry."

Later that year, Mercury released Blow's self-titled debut LP, which featured both tracks as well as his third single, "Hard Times," rap's first socio-politically-charged single that would eventually be covered by Run-DMC.

Kurtis Blow reached the top 10 on Billboard's R&B chart, further expanding rap's fan base and establishing Russell Simmons as one of hip-hop's early major players. In a year that saw hip-hop explode onto the national scene, Blow also became the genre's first rapper to launch a major tour, both in the United States and around the world.

RUSH MANAGEMENT

In later years, other rappers under Rush Artist Management moved into the national spotlight. Whodini, LL Cool J, Run-DMC, the Beastie Boys, Jazzy Jeff and the Fresh Prince, and Public Enemy were all successful acts that began under the stewardship of Simmons and his company.

For a number of years, Rush Artist Management was the only company representing hip-hop artists. But, by the mid-1980s, when it became glaringly apparent that rap was not just a flash in the pan, the number of promoters and managers clamoring to sign rappers increased tenfold. Simmons's artists, however, remained loyal. Their manager had a street swagger that the others didn't. The young entrepreneur walked like them, spoke like them, dressed like them, and attacked the industry game with just as much vigor, if not more.

A Pioneering Partnership

By 1984, Russell Simmons was making good money and building a sound foundation in hip-hop with the nation-wide success of rap artist Kurtis Blow, whose first single, "Christmas Rappin'," and subsequent self-titled album were now being heard all over the country. Simmons, however, had even bigger aspirations for himself and the entire rap genre. "I'm sick of making people rich," he told a colleague one day, according to his autobiography. "I want to own my own . . . record label, my own movie company."

With those ideas swirling in his head, Simmons began look-ing for a partner to help him reach that next level. A mentor once told him that in any new venture, he should first seek out "a 'rabbi' who has the business acumen to help understand the mechanics of that industry," noted Simmons in *Black Enterprise:*

Titans of the B.E. 100s. Simmons desperately needed someone who knew the ins and outs of running a record label.

The previous year, Simmons had bought a record from rappers T La Rock and Jazzy Jay titled "It's Yours." Digging the freshness of the sound, Simmons immediately hunted down the producer of the track by referencing the notes printed on the label: It read "Def Jam in association with Partytime/Streetwise Records."

Simmons was particularly intrigued by the title "Def Jam," which in street terminology meant "good song." Dubbing "It's Yours" as the "blackest" song he had ever heard, Simmons quickly sought out the man responsible for the beat, only to find that the producer was a wealthy white Jewish kid from Long Island operating Def Jam out of his dorm room at New York University.

ENTER RICK RUBIN

Frederick Jay Rubin, who went by the name Rick Rubin, grew up immersed in the angry, rebellious world of hard-rock and punk-rock music, listening to such acts as AC/DC, Aerosmith, Black Flag, and the Germs. Eventually, he was drawn to the similar themes and tones expressed within the burgeoning world of hip-hop, which, according to a 2006 *Washington Post* article, Rubin referred to as "black punk rock."

An outcast in high school who wore black leather and sunglasses, Rubin entered NYU with plans to eventually go to law school. His father, Mickey, worked in the wholesale shoe business; his mother, Linda, joined her husband in hopes that their only child would someday become a lawyer.

When hip-hop began to emerge in the late 1970s and early 1980s, Rubin found himself thinking less and less of his studies. The one-time guitarist in a hard-rock band began dabbling in the production of hip-hop beats. The endeavor was partly inspired by a profound disappointment in the studio recordings that were being released at the time—they contained

In 1984, college student Rick Rubin (*left,* with actor Blair Underwood) cofounded Def Jam Recording with Russell Simmons in Rubin's NYU dorm room. The two made an unlikely pair, but their partnership was a success. Def Jam Recordings became the leading record label for hip-hop music. Rubin went on to produce such diverse recording artists as Justin Timberlake, U2, and Johnny Cash.

mostly looped sections of popular disco records. "And most of them were not good," Rubin told the *Washington Post.* "I wondered what it would be like if a record felt and sounded like being at a club instead of trying to sound like a record."

Stripping away the glossiness of such production, Rubin stuck to simple drum beats, scratches, and little else for "It's Yours." Within two months of its release, the record had caught fire in and around New York. But, more importantly, it had lured a young hip-hop promoter and manager to Rubin's NYU doorstep.

It didn't take long for Simmons and Rubin to realize that a record label partnership—with Simmons providing the talent and Rubin supplying the beats through his already-established Def Jam enterprise—just might be a lucrative situation for both parties. With Simmons and Rubin each contributing $4,000 in seed money, Def Jam Records was officially launched in 1984 from Room 712 of NYU's Weinstein Hall.

Meanwhile, in St. Albans, Queens, a troubled young teen by the name of James Todd Smith was using hip-hop as a way to escape from the problems rampant in his household. He had seen his father shoot his mother and endured the constant physical abuse of his new stepfather. Smith let out his aggressions on the microphone and found solace in the hard edge of the beats underneath MC rhymes. Aching to become a hip-hop artist himself, Smith routinely sent demo tapes to the addresses listed on the rap records he purchased. After picking up "It's Yours," he promptly sent his material to Def Jam under his rap moniker LL Cool J (or Ladies Love Cool James), but the tape ended up sitting for weeks among a pile of cassettes in Rubin's NYU dorm room.

Adam Horowitz, who later went by the name King Ad-Rock as part of the Beastie Boys, was lounging in Rubin's room one day when he came across LL's tape. Horowitz popped it into a cassette deck and took a listen. Blown away by the young man's confident style and delivery, he convinced Rubin and Simmons that the kid should be signed to Def Jam. Before the close of 1984, LL Cool J was not only signed as the label's first artist, but his Rubin-produced first single, "I Need A Beat"—produced for only $700—became a hit record with sales of over 100,000 records.

Simmons had also recruited Rubin to work on a new album by Run-DMC, featuring his brother Joseph "Run" Simmons,

LL Cool J *(center)* was the first artist signed to the Def Jam label. One of the first hip-hop artists to be heavily played on the radio and MTV, LL is still making music today, in addition to acting in films and on television.

Joseph's friend Darryl "DMC" McDaniels, and DJ Jason "Jam Master Jay" Mizell. The trio was already an underground presence with such hits as "It's Like That," "Hard Times," and "Sucker MCs" through their self-titled debut album on Profile Records, launched five years before Def Jam in New York City.

Still managed by Simmons, Run-DMC teamed with Rubin for the follow-up album "Raising Hell," which spawned the hit single "Walk this Way," a rap remake of an Aerosmith rock tune. The song, featuring Aerosmith redoing their music and vocals, was credited with fusing rap and rock and crossing hip-hop into the mainstream. The album went on to become the highest selling rap LP at the time, and its video became the first rap video to appear in heavy rotation on MTV.

With the success of Run-DMC on Profile and LL's "I Need A Beat" on Def Jam, major record labels were finally beginning to admit that hip-hop was more than just a fad. Columbia/CBS Records turned to Simmons and Rubin with an offer to distribute the Def Jam label in a deal worth $600,000. Under the pact, Simmons and Rubin would continue signing talent and producing records for the label, and CBS would take care of the business end of things—including distribution, marketing, and promotion. Def Jam would in turn receive royalties on record sales.

Simmons and Rubin accepted the offer from Columbia/CBS, and suddenly the pair found themselves at the helm of a record label with the ability to reach fans from coast to coast.

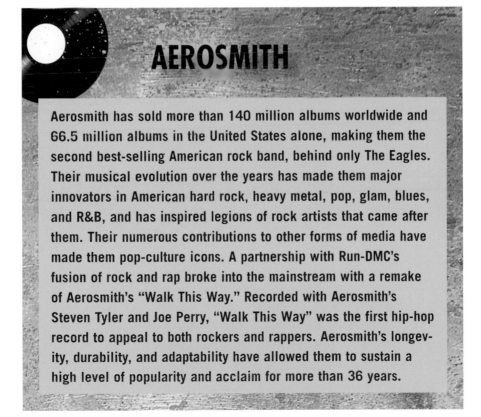

AEROSMITH

Aerosmith has sold more than 140 million albums worldwide and 66.5 million albums in the United States alone, making them the second best-selling American rock band, behind only The Eagles. Their musical evolution over the years has made them major innovators in American hard rock, heavy metal, pop, glam, blues, and R&B, and has inspired legions of rock artists that came after them. Their numerous contributions to other forms of media have made them pop-culture icons. A partnership with Run-DMC's fusion of rock and rap broke into the mainstream with a remake of Aerosmith's "Walk This Way." Recorded with Aerosmith's Steven Tyler and Joe Perry, "Walk This Way" was the first hip-hop record to appeal to both rockers and rappers. Aerosmith's longevity, durability, and adaptability have allowed them to sustain a high level of popularity and acclaim for more than 36 years.

Slick Rick is trailed by the Keystone Cops in this still from his 1989 "Children's Story" video. Slick Rick was a popular rapper in the 1980s who was signed to Def Jam Recordings. Born in England, Slick Rick moved with his family to the Bronx when he was just 10-years-old. It was there that he made a name for himself as a talented rapper, and went on to create the popular songs, "La Di Da Di" and "Children's Story."

"We thought we were living large," Simmons told *Black Enterprise: Titans of the B.E. 100s.* "I made my first $300,000. I was actually more excited about that milestone than when I made my first million years later. I was young and, up to that point, had made no more than $30,000 a year with the promotion business."

With their sudden influx of cash, the two decided to move operations from Rubin's dorm room into a three-story office building in Greenwich Village. Rush Management was located on the first floor, while Def Jam was housed on the second. Rubin had living quarters on the third floor. There was also enough money coming in for Simmons to hire a staff.

Meanwhile, Rubin had produced LL Cool J's debut album, *Radio,* and it was one of the biggest selling rap albums in 1985. Rubin had also produced *Licensed to Ill* by the Beastie Boys, a trio of white kids that included Rubin's friend Horowitz, the kid who first came across LL Cool J's demo tape in Rubin's dorm room. *Licensed to Ill,* a fusion of punk rock, rock, and hip-hop, fueled by its first single "(You Gotta) Fight for Your Right (To Party)," became the first rap record to reach No. 1 on *Billboard's* rap chart. It remains the group's highest selling LP, and in 1985, further cemented Def Jam's dominance within the hip-hop industry.

In the following years, Def Jam experienced what would later be referred to as its "Golden Era," releasing albums from Slick Rick, Public Enemy, and 3rd Bass, among others. Meanwhile, Simmons' Rush Management continued to handle the white-hot careers of Run-DMC at Profile Records, as well as Whodini and DJ Jazzy Jeff and the Fresh Prince over at Jive Records. Simmons had achieved his dream of becoming an influential figure within the world of hip-hop. Soon, however, a rift formed between Simmons and his Def Jam partner that threatened to dismantle his lifelong dream.

Blazing a Hip-Hop Trail

During the late 1980s, Def Jam artists and rappers under Russell Simmons' Rush Management dominated the rap scene. The Beastie Boys' *Licensed to Ill*, released in 1985, sold 5 million copies and became the biggest selling album at the time for Def Jam's distributor, CBS/Columbia. LL Cool J's second Def Jam album, *Bigger and Deffer*, went double platinum in 1987, and by the end of the decade, rap music—once written off as a fad—accounted for approximately 5 percent of all music sales.

The Rush Management act Whodini was a top seller for Jive Records, which signed the group in 1982. The trio, consisting of Jalil (Jalil Hutchins), Ecstasy (John Fletcher), and Grandmaster Dee (Drew Carter), relied on more funk-driven, synthesizer-heavy tracks for such hits as "Friends," "The Freaks Come Out At Night," "One Love," and "Big Mouth." Their 1980s albums: *Whodini* (1983), *Escape* (1984), and *Back in Black* (1986) placed the trio among Run-DMC, LL Cool J, and the Fat Boys as the most successful rap acts of the era.

JAZZY JEFF AND THE FRESH PRINCE: AN INVENTOR AND A STORYTELLER

Meanwhile, a rap duo out of Philadelphia named Jazzy Jeff and the Fresh Prince caught the attention of Simmons with their song, "Girls Ain't Nothing But Trouble," a local hit released in 1985 on Philadelphia-based Pop Art Records. The song's breezy tales of misadventures with the opposite sex—using a sample from the theme song to TV's "I Dream of Jeannie"— had brought local fame to group members DJ Jazzy Jeff (Jeff Townes) and rapper Fresh Prince (Will Smith).

Townes had already made a name for himself as the inventor of a DJ scratching technique called "transforming," in which he periodically tapped the mixing console's crossfader lever open and closed while scratching the record. Smith, meanwhile, was known throughout Philly for skills in the art of storytelling. Simmons quickly added the duo to his Rush Management roster and signed them to Jive Records. Their 1987 debut, *Rock the House,* included "Girls Ain't Nothing But Trouble" and two other releases: "Magnificent Jazzy Jeff" and "Touch Of Jazz."

The album went gold and made them stars on MTV, which paved the way for the group's multi-platinum 1988 follow-up, *He's the DJ, I'm the Rapper.* The set's first single, "Parents Just Don't Understand," became the first rap single to win a Grammy Award. After *Rock the House,* Jazzy Jeff and the Fresh Prince soon found themselves on the Simmons-launched Def Jam 87 Tour, featuring fellow Rush Management act Eric B. and Rakim, and Def Jam artists LL Cool J and socially conscious rap outfit Public Enemy (P.E.).

Hip-hop duo DJ Jazzy Jeff (Jeff Townes, *left*) and the Fresh Prince (Will Smith, *right*) were the first rap artists to receive a Grammy Award, for their single, "Parents Just Don't Understand." The hit rap group was part of Russell Simmons's Rush Artist Management and was signed on for the Def Jam '87 Tour. The tour featured popular Rush Management and Def Jam Artists such as LL Cool J and Public Enemy.

PUBLIC ENEMY

Based in Long Island, P.E. was fronted by Chuck D (Carlton Ridenhour), his jovial sidekick Flavor Flav (William Drayton), road manager and occasional vocalist Professor Griff (Richard Griffin), and DJ Terminator X (Norman Rogers). P.E. released its first album, *Yo! Bum Rush the Show,* in 1987, a year after Rubin signed the group to Def Jam based on a demo of Chuck D freestyling. Using a distinct mesh of cacophonous sounds and samples by producers The Bomb Squad (Hank and Keith Shocklee, Bill Stephany, and Eric "Vietnam" Sadler), the in-your-face attitude of the album was reflected through such singles as "Miuzi Weighs a Ton" and "Public Enemy No. 1."

While label mates LL Cool J, Whodini and Rush Management acts Eric B. and Rakim and Jazzy Jeff and The Fresh Prince received more adulation from hip-hop fans during the U.S. leg of the Def Jam 87 Tour, the overseas audiences belonged to Public Enemy, with crowds often finding kinship in the rebellious nature of Chuck D's fiery lyrics.

Chuck D explained in an entry at PublicEnemy.com on May 1, 2003, "Initially the first audiences who understood us were non-black ones that compared us to the [punk group] Clash of ten years prior. I saw in the Rush Management offices gigantic boxes of fan mail for the other groups, and loads of unanswered requests for interviews [for P.E.], especially from across the seas in Europe, the UK and Japan. . . . Thus, even before we continued the Def Jam tour overseas there was buzz built through the press. This led to hype and build-up that completely caught our tour partners LL and Eric B by surprise."

It wasn't until their second album in 1988, *It Takes a Nation of Millions to Hold Us Back,* that Public Enemy caught on among black audiences in the United States and cemented itself as a revolutionary rap act with opinions on the state of black America. Songs such as "Don't Believe the Hype," "Black Steel in the Hour of Chaos," "Bring the Noise," and "Night of

Public Enemy (*from left*: Chuck D, Terminator X, and Flavor Flav) was a socially conscious rap group that changed the face of rap music and expanded the hip-hop community globally. Chuck D's controversial lyrics affected and inspired in hit songs such as "Bring the Noise" and "Fight the Power." Public Enemy was one of Def Jam's most popular groups.

the Living Baseheads" were embraced by music journalists. It was voted Album of the Year by the *Village Voice* Pazz and Jop Poll and became the first hip-hop album to earn a number one ranking by predominantly rock critics.

P.E.'s fiery lyrics and innovative beats were still too unconventional for urban radio outlets, which, in large part, turned down Simmons's requests to insert P.E. singles into regular rotation. According to *Black Enterprise Titans of the B.E. 100s*, Simmons resorted to the tactics used in his college days of promoting rap shows to drum up interest in the group's third album, *Fear of a Black Planet*. He began sending out young street teams to put up posters, billboards, and stickers of the album on public surfaces. Simmons also met with nightclub

SLICK RICK THE RULER

Another Def Jam artist to enjoy success in the 1980s was Slick Rick, a London-born, Bronx-bred rapper who went platinum in 1988 with his debut album, *The Great Adventures of Slick Rick.*

Born Richard Walters in South Wimbledon, Slick Rick (a.k.a. Ricky D. or Rick the Ruler), set himself apart from other rap acts by wearing a patch over his right eye. The eye was blinded from a childhood injury involving broken glass. In 1975, when he was 10, Slick Rick moved with his family to the Bronx, where in the 1980s he began winning MC contests on the local rap circuit.

Soon, he was introduced to rapper/beat-boxer Doug E. Fresh, who teamed with the Brit in the summer of 1985 for the hits "La Di Da Di" and "The Show." The tracks inspired Simmons to offer Rick a deal. The 1988 release of *The Great Adventures of Slick Rick* featured several singles that became hip-hop classics, including "Teenage Love," "Hey Young World," and one of the most enduring cuts in rap history, "Children's Story." But he was unable to capitalize on its success. Three years later, Slick Rick was convicted of attempted murder after shooting his cousin and a bystander. Russell Simmons bailed him out of jail and rushed the recording of his sophomore album, *The Ruler's Back,* before the artist was sentenced to prison, where he remained for the next five years.

DJs and program directors at college radio stations and got them to add to their playlists tracks from *Fear of a Black Planet,* including the anthem "Fight the Power," "Welcome to the Terrordome," and the Flavor Flav-led "911 Is a Joke."

Simmons's grassroots promotion and marketing proved successful, as *Fear of a Black Planet* sold 500,000 copies within 10 days of its release in 1989. Going into the new decade, Public Enemy had become Def Jam's top-selling act—both in the States and abroad.

SEVERING TIES

With platinum-selling rap artists and successful international tours, Def Jam seemed unstoppable in the late 1980s. But a crack in the armor would soon make itself known through escalating creative differences between Simmons and Rick Rubin. They reached a peak during renegotiations with Columbia/ CBS records—which in 1988 had been acquired by Sony and renamed Sony Music Entertainment. Simmons wanted to restructure the deal to take advantage of Sony's corporate influence and expand Def Jam into other businesses. "I was a manager and I wanted to establish new venues for my acts," Simmons told *Black Enterprise.* "I knew I couldn't do it without a company like Sony."

Rubin, however, thought it was important for the hip-hop label to maintain as much independence as possible. This sentiment was also mixed with a growing frustration over Lyor Cohen, a former road manager for Run-DMC and longtime Def Jam employee, whom Simmons had just promoted to the position of president.

Rubin decided he didn't like the direction Def Jam was going and severed ties with Simmons in 1988, ending one of the most influential partnerships in music history. In severing ties, the two executives split Def Jam's assets, with Simmons maintaining the Def Jam name, logo, and artists—excluding the Beastie Boys. Citing royalty issues, the famous trio also left

Lyor Cohen *(right)* began his career as Run-DMC's road manager. From there he became a longtime employee of Def Jam, managing tours and working with Rush Artist Management. When Russell Simmons promoted Cohen to president of Def Jam, it was a cause of contention between Simmons and Rick Rubin. In 1988, Simmons and Rubin ended their successful partnership, with Rubin leaving Def Jam Recordings.

Def Jam in 1989 and signed with Capitol Records to release their critically acclaimed second album, *Paul's Boutique.*

In 1989, Rubin teamed with Time Warner to launch his own rock label, Def American, in a deal reported to be worth between $75 million and $100 million, according to the *Washington Post.* It was also during this time that Will Smith decided to leave Rush Management. The rapper's exit, however, proved lucrative for Simmons due to the timing of Smith's impending sitcom deal with NBC. As noted in Simmons's book *Life and Def,* Smith was still with Rush Management when Simmons took the charismatic rapper to Hollywood in search of a film and television deal. Meetings with executives Jon Peters and Peter Guber of Sony-owned Columbia Pictures, however, did not yield any deals.

Perhaps feeling limited by Simmons's allegiance to Sony, Smith took meetings privately with other parties. As Simmons recalls in *Life and Def,* Smith was pitched by Quincy Jones and "an ambitious young Warner Bros. A&R executive named Benny Medina" to star in a TV sitcom based loosely on Medina's life. "Then they went to Quincy's house to close the deal for the *Fresh Prince of Bel Air,* while I flew home on the red eye unaware." The following day, Simmons said, Smith called him with an offer of $250,000 to be released from his management contract—a payment Simmons decided to accept. Although Simmons would have made even more money if Smith had stayed by him, he did benefit from the large release check.

With Will Smith, the Beastie Boys, and Rick Rubin gone, Simmons set about paving the way for Def Jam's future. He and Lyor Cohen promptly met with Sony to restructure their distribution deal. In 1990, the two parties made history by brokering the first-ever joint venture between a rap label and an entertainment company, in which earnings would be split 50-50. (In the old pact, the former Columbia/CBS kept all of the profits and paying a royalty fee to Def Jam for each release.) The new Sony deal also called for the conglomerate to pay Def Jam $3 million for operating expenses.

Once again, Russell Simmons was back on top of the rap game, having positioned himself and his artists under Def Jam and Rush Management to capitalize on all that hip-hop success had to offer, including movies, television, and the art form's next lucrative frontier, marketing.

Endorsing My Adidas

During the '80s I spent most of my time promoting hip-hop as music—during the '90s I used that success to expand the reach of hip-hop culture.

—Russell Simmons

By the mid-1980s, hip-hop—once feared by Madison Avenue—had no problem cozying up to the influence of corporate America. Even "Rapper's Delight," the song that exposed most of the world to hip hop for the first time in 1979, gives a shout-out to Lincoln Continental cars and the Holiday Inn hotel chain. But it would be seven more years before the walls between hip-hop and commerce were kicked down with authority by Run-DMC.

"My Adidas," the trio's 1986 hit single from the LP *Raising Hell,* was an ode to the popular tennis shoe made by

Germany's Adidas-Salomon AG. The song, which peaked at No. 5 on Billboard's R&B chart, is credited as one of the first rap records to promote a product within its lyrics—which included the lines:

> Now the Adidas I possess for one man is rare
> Myself homeboy got 50 pair
> Got blue and black cause I like to chill
> And yellow and green when it's time to get ill

Russell Simmons also understood the impact of hip-hop and its ability to give instant consumer appeal to any product the rap artist chose to drop into his rhymes. Sensing a way to capitalize on the increasing corporate interest in hip-hop, Simmons came up with the idea of approaching Adidas to sign Run-DMC to an endorsement deal.

In a 2002 interview with VH1.com, Darryl "DMC" McDaniels said Simmons thought of the record's Adidas concept one day while standing on Hollis Avenue. "He was like, 'What can these guys rhyme about next? I know, my Adidas!' " Simmons said. "He stood there for two hours ranting and raving about this Adidas record to us. 'Y'all gotta make a record about where your sneakers have been!' Once Russell gave us the idea, Run and me ran with it." Simmons explained that in their day, wearing Adidas without shoestrings—the group's preferred way to sport the sneakers—signified that one had been in jail, "because when you were in jail they would take your laces so you wouldn't hang yourself. The whole premise behind that was how Run-DMC can turn something that was negative into a positive image."

Once the song became a hit, Simmons sat down with executives from Adidas and pitched the company the idea of cashing in on Run-DMC's ability to sell Adidas sneakers through the popularity of the trio's hit single. Simmons extolled the virtues of having a popular rap act promoting the shoes, which would set them apart from competitors Nike and Reebok, which

In 1986, rap group Run-DMC produced the hit single "My Adidas," an ode to the popular tennis shoe. In his quest to bring hip-hop culture to the forefront of mainstream media, Russell Simmons organized the first-ever endorsement deal for a rap artist, partnering Run-DMC with Adidas. More than twenty years later, the group (*left to right*: Run, the late Jam Master Jay, and DMC) is still associated with the shoes.

employed top athletes to sell their products. In light of today's shoe endorsement deals with such rap acts as The Game and Jay-Z, Adidas execs should have immediately jumped at the chance to capitalize on Run-DMC's Adidas connection. But, in 1986, Simmons found himself fighting an uphill battle. At the end of the meeting with Simmons, the Adidas executives were not convinced that a deal with a hip-hop act would be in the best interest of the sports-apparel company.

Simmons, however, would not take "no" for an answer. He managed to convince the suits to attend the next Run-DMC concert at New York's Madison Square Garden and witness for themselves the group's powerful influence over their consumer base. As the story goes, the businessmen stood patiently among the young crowd waiting for the song "My Adidas" to be performed. DMC explained the moment to VH1.com: "Me and Run used to do this thing where Run would say, 'I tried to get

THE IMPORTANCE OF SNEAKERS IN HIP-HOP CULTURE

Senegal-born film director Thibaut De Longeville, who includes a segment on the importance of "My Adidas" in his documentary *Just for Kicks,* explains the importance of hip-hop's global influence in an interview with the *Montreal Mirror. Just For Kicks* is the first documentary film examining the history of the sneaker phenomena within hip-hop culture. Several rap artists, journalists, brand marketers, and other sneaker addicts were interviewed for the film. These industry players share their passion and their perspectives on how and why sneakers have evolved into one of the key elements of style of the MTV generation.

De Longville told the *Montreal Mirror* that during the 1970s, "ninety-nine per cent of sneaker sales were athletic, and one per cent was what companies consider 'lifestyle.' Nowadays, athletic purchases make up only about twenty per cent of the market." According to De Longville, hip-hop made them a staple of culture: "Even though we were not from the U.S., we were wearing Pumas because of Rock Steady Crew, we were wearing Adidas because of Run-DMC and the Beastie Boys, and we were in Jordans because of Public Enemy and N.W.A. and Spike Lee's movies," he says. "It was somehow a symbol of our culture."

in here and a security guard told me, "You can't come in here you thug." So I said, "I'm Run-DMC and these are my Adidas."' When [we] said that, we put our Adidas up in the air. Everyone in the whole sold-out Garden held their Adidas up."

One of the representatives from the German company who witnessed the crowd lift their Adidas sneakers en masse approached Simmons immediately to voice the company's enthusiasm about an endorsement deal with the rap trio. "We didn't know the representatives from Adidas were there," DMC told the *Village Voice* in 2002. "But when [Russell] saw that, he ran backstage and said, 'I'm going to get you guys an endorsement contract.'" Soon after the concert, Adidas-Salomon AG offered Run-DMC $1.5 million to endorse Adidas, marking the first time in history that a shoe company employed nonathletes to promote their product.

Launched in the United States in 1969 as a basketball shoe, the Adidas sneaker was suddenly available nearly 20 years later as a Run-DMC version complete with the trio's logo on the side of the heel. Adidas also agreed to sponsor the rest of the group's "Raising Hell" Tour. It was also around this time that Simmons secured another hip-hop milestone for his Rush Management artist Kurtis Blow.

Already in history books as the first rapper to sign a major-label deal, the first to score a gold single ("The Breaks"), and the first rapper to embark on a concert tour, Blow actually preceded Run-DMC as the first rap artist to sign an endorsement contract. In 1985, Blow starred in national commercial ads for the soft drink Sprite, thanks to a deal brokered by his manager, Russell Simmons.

THE FIRST HIP-HOP MOVIE

Simmons's uncanny ability to exploit revenue-making opportunities within hip-hop was also felt 3,000 miles away under the bright lights of Hollywood. In 1985, he produced the world's first hip-hop-themed film, *Krush Groove,* which was loosely

The 1985 film *Krush Groove* was loosely based on the early years of Def Jam Recordings. Produced by Russell Simmons, the film featured many Def Jam artists such as LL Cool J, Run-DMC, the Beastie Boys, and *(pictured)* The Fat Boys. Although the film was a box-office success, Simmons was not completely satisfied with the movie-making experience.

based on the launch of Def Jam and starred many of the artists on its roster—including LL Cool J, Run-DMC, the Beastie Boys, Kurtis Blow, and even Rick Rubin as himself. Simmons, aware of his limitations as an actor, hired Blair Underwood to portray Russell Walker, the character based on himself. Percussionist Sheila E. starred as his love interest.

MENDELIAN INHERITANCE

AUTOSOMAL RECESSIVE
AUTOSOMAL DOMINANT
X-LINKED
POLYGENIC

$dd\ H_2O = 5.0\ mL$
$20\%\ PEG = 0.5\ m$
$20x\ SSPE = 1.0\ m$
$20\%\ SDS = 3.5$

Russell Simmons continued his foray into filmmaking, producing the hit 1996 movie, *The Nutty Professor.* **The film was a remake of the popular 1963 Jerry Lewis vehicle of the same name and featured comedian Eddie Murphy** *(above).*

Directed by Michael Schultz, who had also directed the Berry Gordy-produced *The Last Dragon* in 1985, *Krush Groove* was budgeted at $3 million, but went on to gross $15 million at the box office. Simmons's first stab at moviemaking was a success, but he wasn't completely satisfied with his first foray into Tinseltown. There were creative clashes between Simmons and Schultz over the film's content, battles that were always won by the director.

"There were a lot of scenes that embarrassed us. They were too bubble-gum," Simmons explained in his book *Life and Def:*

Sex, Drugs, Money + God. The experience soured him on film-making. But three years later, he tried his luck again with *Tougher Than Leather,* described as a grittier, more street film that was closer to what Simmons had envisioned for *Krush Groove.*

After viewing Spike Lee's 1988 film *School Daze,* Simmons offered the director the chance to direct *Tougher Than Leather.* But Lee declined, opting instead to shoot his own film, *Do The Right Thing.* So, Rubin took on the director's role to ensure that their original vision would not be compromised. The story centered on Run-DMC and its harassment by a group of gangsters. The Beastie Boys, Slick Rick, Rubin, and even Russell Simmons served as costars, but their presence wasn't enough to lure distribution offers early on. Finally, Simmons was able to sell the rights to New Line Cinema, which released the film in 1988 to abysmal reviews. Budgeted at $700,000, the film did earn a profit with a box office take of $3 million. But Simmons was not given any portion of the profits. Again, his dalliance with Hollywood left a bitter taste. It would take another seven years for Simmons to approach the movie business again, as an executive producer with the Abel Ferrara-directed film *The Addiction* in 1995 and the box office hit *The Nutty Professor* the following year.

In the meantime, Simmons had begun setting his sights on the invasion of yet another industry, bringing his hip-hop swagger and business acumen to the world of high fashion.

Phat Fashionista

By 1991, Russell Simmons was riding high and making millions of dollars through his record label, Def Jam. The company had 10 gold, 6 platinum, and 2 multiplatinum records that year, generating 60 percent ($21 million) of Simmons's annual revenues. The entrepreneur didn't let the company's success lull him into complacency, however. Still driven to take the hip-hop culture in new directions, Simmons prepared by organizing his numerous ventures under one multimedia conglomerate, Rush Communications.

The goal of this new venture was to develop various businesses that could market hip-hop to mainstream consumers. According to the company's manifesto, each business under Rush Communications would "reach out to its particular niche and dominate that market. Together, the businesses would help to develop interconnected marketing and advertising plans for a broad and varied audience—ultimately, helping to define generations." The obvious first company to be housed under the new conglomerate was Def Jam Records, which in the early 1990s continued to churn out hits from Public Enemy, LL Cool J, and Slick Rick. Soon, however, Def Jam was joined by a number of disparate ventures that would push hip-hop into the unlikeliest of places.

It was also in the early nineties that Simmons began turning his attention to the fashion industry. With more and more hip-hop artists dropping the names of such labels as Gucci, Polo, and Tommy Hilfiger into their lyrics, the Def Jam mogul saw another money-making opportunity.

Simmons takes credit for suggesting that fashion designer Tommy Hilfiger take advantage of his label's popularity within the hip-hop community. He introduced Hilfiger to rap stars, who in turn joined models in sporting his gear during runway shows. Eventually, Hilfiger's street credibility skyrocketed, which in turn helped to boost the designer's profits.

Eventually, Simmons figured he could start his own fashion label and market hip-hop-inspired clothing to the same demographic. In 1992, he founded Phat Farm, a men's sportswear brand that featured All-American-style clothing such as T-shirts, denim and preppy urban outerwear, loungewear, and footwear.

PHAT FARM CLOTHING LINE

Phat Farm did not show a profit for six years, but the line's T-shirts and jeans became instantly popular among urban youths. As the company continued to build, Simmons grew more and more frustrated with the fashion industry's somewhat myopic response to his label. According to Simmons, some factions of the industry relegated his line under the title "ethnic," a categorization he felt was flat out wrong and misleading.

"I don't classify my clothing as an ethnic line. I mean, my biggest seller is a pink golf sweater," he was quoted as saying in *Black Enterprise Titans of the B.E. 100s*. "It's not a dashiki or a grass skirt. I don't accept the concept of ethnic clothing. We have the same quality as Tommy Hilfiger or Ralph Lauren. I don't know what's ethnic about our clothing except that I'm ethnic and I own it. We don't want to have our products, whether it's film, fashion, or a magazine, pigeonholed. African-American culture is mainstream. It's what the world has come to see as American. We want to fully participate in its marketing like every other company."

Simmons had a strategy to circumvent the challenges of being segregated by department stores, and that was to keep his product as far away from them as possible. Simmons instead made his line available to small specialty shops during its early years, choosing to build his distribution slowly and methodically.

His plan worked like a charm. Soon momentum built and department stores began begging for Phat Farm apparel. What began as a $500,000 boutique brand blossomed into a $510 million lifestyle brand that included apparel, jewelry, eyewear, loungewear, fragrance, footwear, suits, and other accessories. In adherence to his own rules, Simmons immersed himself in the world of fashion and made a point to hobnob with experts in the field who could serve as mentors. A year after launching Phat Farm, Simmons attended a fashion show for Karl Lagerfeld and found himself enamored by the designer's muse, a 5-foot-11, 17-year-old model named Kimora Lee.

Born in St. Louis to a Japanese mother, Joanne "Kyoko" Perkins, and an African-American father, Vernon Whitlock Jr., the young beauty was flattered when Simmons, then 35, ventured backstage specifically to meet her. "She told me that she was 18. Her mother said it was okay if we dated," Simmons told *Ebony* magazine in 2003. "She had lived all over the world. She

Russell Simmons met supermodel Kimora Lee in 1992 at a Karl Lagerfeld fashion show. They dated for five years and married in 1998. Kimora and Russell have two daughters, Ming Lee Simmons and Aoki Lee Simmons. In 2006, Russell and Kimora announced the end of their marriage.

spoke a bunch of languages, French, German, Italian, Japanese. She had a certain polish and sophistication."

Despite the age difference, Simmons and Lee dated for five years before exchanging wedding vows in St. Barthelemy during a lavish ceremony on December 20, 1998, that drew the likes of lifestyle guru Martha Stewart and then Arista Records executive Clive Davis.

Russell's brother Joseph "Run" Simmons had become a born-again Christian and presided over the ceremony under his new moniker, Rev Run. Among Lee's bridesmaids, who wore lavender chiffon, were fellow models Tyra Banks and Veronica Webb. Lee wore a white gown by Susan Lazar, while Simmons stood at the altar in Phat Farm casual wear and a pair of Adidas. His groomsmen, including his brother Danny, former Motown head Andre Harrell, and Lyor Cohen, wore Phat Farm khaki slacks, oxford shirts, and golf sweaters.

Two years into their marriage, Kimora ended up in charge of a women's arm of her husband's Phat Farm collection. Simmons had begun printing a promotional line of baby T-shirts that he named Baby Phat. Female models wore these tees during Phat Farm runway shows to add spice to the runway experience. When models and celebrities began sporting the limited collection shirts on the streets, Russell sensed another opportunity to make money.

In 2000, Simmons officially launched an entire Baby Phat collection of women's clothing and hired Kimora to be the line's creative director. The collection soon supplemented its T-shirts with such garments as metallic pink miniskirts, furry white go-go boots, and leopard-print tops. Eventually, the line expanded to include cocktail dresses, outerwear, shoes, and a line for youngsters titled Phat Kids Collection.

By 1992, Rush Communications was beginning to take shape in the way that Simmons had envisioned. With Def Jam, Phat Farm, and Baby Phat in the stable, Simmons started looking to other industries to conquer.

In the photograph above, Kimora Lee Simmons struts down the runway with her daughter, Ming Lee Simmons, at the 2002 Baby Phat Fall fashion show. In 2000, Russell Simmons launched the women's line for Baby Phat Clothing and assigned Kimora as the creative director.

BREAKING INTO FILM—AGAIN

The mogul focused his attention on addressing the 45.3 million minority consumers who were spending $12.6 billion annually in urban-themed entertainment. Simmons saw an opening to bring hip-hop sensibilities into the world of film and television. By developing urban-themed projects to take advantage of the growing influence of hip-hop in mainstream American culture, Simmons felt he could blaze a trail in delivering innovative and quality programming featuring young up-and-coming urban artists.

Obeying his own rule of teaming with experts who know more than he does in a particular field, Simmons joined forces with veteran television producer and director Stan Lathan, the father of actress Sanaa Lathan and director of such African-American sitcoms as *Sanford and Son, Amen, Frank's Place, True Colors, Roc, Martin, South Central, Moesha,* and *The Steve Harvey Show.*

Together, Simmons and Lathan addressed the severe lack of urban content on the big and small screens by founding the production company Simmons Lathan Entertainment, which set as its goal the development of television series, specials, movies, and live entertainment.

While hanging at comedy clubs along Los Angeles's Crenshaw Boulevard, Simmons began considering the world of stand-up comedy as his first venture under Simmons Lathan Entertainment.

He was inspired by the late comedian Robin Harris, who used to host nights at the Comedy Act Theater on Crenshaw and became a local legend for his ability to make up jokes on the spot about folks in the audience. He became legendary for his famous comedy routine "Bebe's Kids," in which he took a group of unruly kids from South Central to Disneyland.

Together, Simmons and Lathan attempted to develop a television project or feature film for Harris, but those plans stopped abruptly in March of 1990 when the Chicago-born comedian died

Television producer and director Stan Lathan *(left)*, his daughter actress Sanaa Lathan *(center)*, and Russell Simmons (*right*) are photographed in 2003. Simmons and Stan Lathan formed Simmons Lathan Entertainment to produce urban content for television and film. Simmons Lathan Entertainment produced *Def Comedy Jam*, and its spinoff *Def Poetry Jam*, which aired on HBO.

of a heart attack. Harris' death, however, did not stop Simmons' plan to bring stand-up comedy into Rush Communications. Sensing that black comedy was exploding in such cities as Los Angeles, New York, Washington, D.C., and Baltimore, Simmons felt he could develop a series that would give these African-American comics a nationwide platform.

Simmons and Lathan teamed with Hollywood producers Bernie Brillstein and Brad Grey of the production company

Brillstein-Gray, the duo that developed *Ghostbusters* and *Wayne's World,* and pitched an idea for a series called *Def Comedy Jam* to HBO.

Hosted by Martin Lawrence, the show would feature African-American stand-up comics performing before a live audience. Rooted in hip-hop culture, the show would have a DJ spinning records at the beginning and end of the program and between acts to hype up the crowd. HBO decided to take a chance on the concept and ordered eight episodes of *Def Comedy Jam* to begin airing in March of 1992.

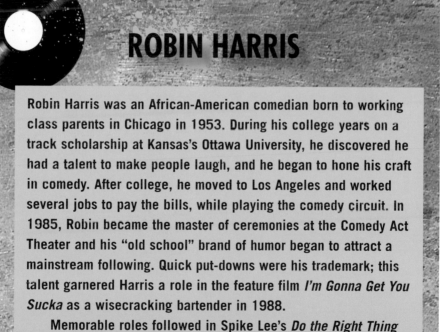

ROBIN HARRIS

Robin Harris was an African-American comedian born to working class parents in Chicago in 1953. During his college years on a track scholarship at Kansas's Ottawa University, he discovered he had a talent to make people laugh, and he began to hone his craft in comedy. After college, he moved to Los Angeles and worked several jobs to pay the bills, while playing the comedy circuit. In 1985, Robin became the master of ceremonies at the Comedy Act Theater and his "old school" brand of humor began to attract a mainstream following. Quick put-downs were his trademark; this talent garnered Harris a role in the feature film *I'm Gonna Get You Sucka* as a wisecracking bartender in 1988.

Memorable roles followed in Spike Lee's *Do the Right Thing* and *Mo' Better Blues,* as well as *Harlem Nights* and *House Party.* Harris was about to strike gold with a feature film version of his popular "Bébé's Kids" comedy routines, when he died suddenly from a heart attack at the age of 36.

Taking Urban Mainstream

In 1991, Simmons began producing *Def Comedy Jam* for HBO through his newly formed Simmons Lathan Entertainment, a media company under his Rush Communications outfit that already featured his label Def Jam Records and his fashion lines Phat Farm and Baby Phat. Hosted by Martin Lawrence and deejayed by popular hip-hop turntablist Kid Capri, the series captured early performances of some of today's most successful comedians, including Chris Tucker, Steve Harvey, Bernie Mac, Jamie Foxx, DL Hughley, and Bill Bellamy.

Def Comedy Jam, with its comics engaging freely in coarse language and vulgar humor, quickly became the highest rated cable show in its Friday night timeslot and developed a reputation of being able to launch successful careers.

"What happened with 'Def Comedy Jam' was that the top comedians working the circuit got even better because they saw the show as a vehicle that could make them stars," Simmons said in his autobiography, *Life & Def.* "An appearance on the show guaranteed them more national bookings."

HBO took notice of the ratings and requested that Simmons increase the initial number of episodes from 8 to 22. The pay-cable channel paid Simmons Lathan Entertainment $2 million to produce all 22 in 1992, but Simmons Lathan was able to make the shows for under $500,000, Simmons noted in his autobiography *Life & Def.*

Simmons was able to keep costs low by hiring comedians for very little money, as most up-and-coming comics were less concerned with pay and more interested in the national exposure *Def Comedy Jam* and HBO had to offer.

THE DEF COMEDY JAM DEAL

The desperation of the comics gave Simmons another idea. He decided to form another enterprise that merged Simmons Lathan with Brillstein-Grey to form Simmons, Lathan, Brillstein and Grey Entertainment (SLBG) with the purpose of managing the careers of Def Jam comics for a 20 percent commission.

Using Creative Artists Agency as a model, SLBG ignored the traditional route of looking for outside projects their clients could join. Instead, the new company created in-house packages that employed talent from each of their businesses. For example, *Def Comedy Jam* comics would appear in film or television products developed under Rush Communications.

In 1993, Simmons organized the first Def Comedy Jam tour, which took several of the comics on the road. The series, meanwhile, stayed on HBO for six seasons before it ended its run in 1996 as one of HBO's highest-rated programs. *Def Comedy Jam* left a legacy of introducing talented black comedians to mainstream American culture.

Def Comedy Jam began airing in 1992. It was hosted by Martin Lawrence and featured up-and-coming comedians such as Chris Tucker, Bernie Mac, and Jamie Foxx. The show became one of HBO's highest rated, and it spawned the Def Comedy Jam tour, which took several of the comics on the road.

DEF POETRY JAM

The show led to a spinoff, *Def Poetry Jam,* in 2002, featuring the nation's top slam poets as well as artists known for their gift of spoken word, including Sonia Sanchez, Nikki Giovanni, and Amiri Baraka. The show's success on HBO led Simmons to invest several million dollars to launch a Broadway version of *Def Poetry Jam.* While it lost money during its New York run, the production earned critical acclaim and a 2003 Tony Award for Best Special Theatrical Event. With such an honor behind it, Simmons took the show overseas to theater houses in Edinburgh and London.

Simmons's idea to launch *Def Comedy Jam* in 1992 would set off a ripple effect of success for years to come. As his television endeavors began to take off in 1994, Simmons's Def Jam label neared the end of its distribution deal with Sony. Seeking to expand his record company even further than its endeavors under Sony, Simmons met with PolyGram CEO Alain Levy and agreed on a deal in which the company would acquire a 50 percent stake in Def Jam Records for $30 million and also facilitate the expansion of Rush Communications into film production. For Simmons, it was worth giving up half of Def Jam to gain a stronger foothold in Hollywood.

Wasting no time in taking advantage of his new arrangement, Simmons began making bigger budget movies the following year and became an executive producer for the 1995 film *Addiction.* Shot in 20 days by director Abel Ferrara, the film starred Lili Taylor as a doctoral student in philosophy who changes her views on the nature of evil and humanity after being bitten by a vampire. *Addiction* was followed up in 1996 by *The Nutty Professor,* produced by Simmons and starring Eddie Murphy in a remake of the 1963 Jerry Lewis comedy. Murphy played multiple characters in the movie about an obese professor, Sherman Klump, who turned into the fit and cocky Buddy Love after taking a special concoction. The film's tremendous crossover success at the box office restored

Russell Simmons Presents Def Poetry was the next venture for Simmons Lathan Entertainment. The show, hosted by Mos Def, featured poets, singers, actors, and artists giving spoken-word performances. Public advocate Mark Green *(left)*, Mos Def *(center)*, and Russell Simmons *(right)* are photographed at the post-premiere party for the show in 2001.

Simmons' faith in Hollywood as a bankable addition to his stable of business ventures.

"When I was making 'The Nutty Professor,' somebody told me no black producer makes mainstream movies," Simmons told *New York* magazine in 1998. "I looked around and there really weren't any. But you have to break the mold and change the mind of even black executives, because that's critical for the success of the culture and of mankind; that's what it's all about."

Also in 1996, Simmons was an associate producer on *The Funeral,* starring Christopher Walken and Chris Penn as brothers dealing with the recent death of their younger brother, played by Vincent Gallo.

In January 1997, Gramercy Pictures released *Gridlock'd* with Simmons, again, serving as an executive producer. The action comedy featured Tupac Shakur in one of his final cinematic performances. Directed by Vonde Curtis Hall, the film starred Tupac and Tim Roth as drug addicts who attempted to kick their habit after a friend overdoses. The movie earned an award for best picture at the esteemed Sundance Film Festival in Aspen, Colorado, and Tupac received great reviews for his role. His potentially bright future in Hollywood, however, was not meant to be. Four months before the release of *Gridlock'd,* Tupac was shot and killed in a drive-by shooting in Las Vegas.

Hip-hop was dealt a major blow with the sudden and tragic death of its biggest star. The genre's rivalry between East and West coast artists—rumored to have played a part in the murder of Tupac and subsequently his rival Notorious B.I.G.— had nearly overshadowed the quiet-but-important cinematic accomplishments Simmons was making in Hollywood.

Simmons's string of films during the 1990s, including the comedy *How to Be A Player* in late 1997, featuring Simmons and Lathan as producers, proved to Hollywood that motion pictures with black actors and urban themes can appeal to all races, and that African Americans can indeed serve as executive producers for movies that target mainstream audiences. In 1994, Simmons took this belief to the publishing world with the creation of *One World* magazine.

"I think that black guys love Arnold Schwarzenegger, and white guys like Snoop Dogg. And I believe black girls want to read about and sleep with Leonardo DiCaprio and that white girls are interested in LL Cool J the same way," Simmons told *New York* magazine.

While continuing to work the Def Jam brand into mainstream America, Simmons also understood that hip-hop was where his bread was buttered, and the continuation of the record label as a major player in rap music was essential for the Def Jam name to preserve its influence. Simmons kept that in mind when Shawn Carter, a young rapper from Brooklyn's Marcy Projects, showed up at his Def Jam offices one day in 1997.

ROC-A-FELLA RECORDS

Like Russell Simmons, Carter was a born hustler, having sold drugs for a time before excessive violence encouraged him to pursue less perilous business ventures. Carter, along with his friends Damon Dash and Kareem "Biggs" Burke, got an idea to start a label named Roc-A-Fella Records, with Carter as its first rap artist, under the name Jay-Z.

With a demo tape and a bag full of cash, Jay-Z, Dash and Burke visited the offices of Def Jam and encountered Kevin Liles, the company's head of promotions. "They came in and said, 'All we want you to do is get our record played,'" Liles recalled to *Fortune* magazine in October 2005. "I said, 'Why don't you sign with us?' And they said, 'No, we have our own company.'"

Turning down their offer, Liles agreed to promote the song instead. The following year, Jay-Z released his first album, *Reasonable Doubt,* and quickly established himself as one of hip-hop's most respected rappers. Based on the album's success, Liles and his boss, Lyor Cohen, were not about to pass up an opportunity to get in business with Roc-A-Fella. Def Jam convinced Jay-Z, Dash, and Burke to sell them a 50 percent stake in the label for $1.5 million.

Two more albums were released by Jay-Z in the next two years. By 1999, the Brooklyn rapper had become a household name, and Def Jam was about to experience another corporate shuffle with its parent company PolyGram, which by then had

In 2004, rap superstar Jay-Z was named president and CEO of Def Jam Records, replacing Lyor Cohen. In 1996, Jay-Z cofounded his own record label, Roc-A-Fella Records, which is still under his control and is now owned by Def Jam.

acquired another 10 percent stake in Def Jam to become 60 percent owners.

JAY-Z FOR PRESIDENT

In 1998, PolyGram was purchased by Seagrams and absorbed into its Universal Music Group, which had become the biggest record company in the world. A year following the acquisition, Universal bought the remaining 40 percent interest in Def Jam and combined it with one of its other labels, Island Records, to form The Island Def Jam Music Group.

Headed by Antonio "L.A." Reid, the label acted on Simmons's idea to form an R&B arm of Def Jam, titled Def Soul. R&B artists Dru Hill and Kelly Price were moved over from Island to join such signed vocalists as Musiq, Montell Jordan, Case, 112, Patti LaBelle, and the Isley Brothers.

As Def Jam continued to grow and expand, Jay-Z sat back and watched Simmons maneuver between his various ventures. As Simmons did with Def Jam, Jay-Z, Dash, and Burke began making moves to establish Roc-A-Fella as a marketable brand with the creation of a Rocawear clothing line, feature films including *Fade to Black* and *State Property,* as well as Jay-Z's 40/40 nightclub and Reebok sneaker line.

The ultimate irony occurred in December 2004, when Jay-Z was named president and CEO of Def Jam records, replacing Lyor Cohen, who had left the company in January of that year to head Warner Music Group. With Jay-Z's arrival, Def Jam also announced that it had purchased the remaining 50 percent of Roc-A-Fella, whose acts included the 10-time Grammy nominee Kanye West, Cam'ron, and Beanie Sigel. Heading into the new millennium, Simmons had built Rush Communications into a major media player that stretched hip-hop and urban culture deep into the homes of mainstream America.

Hip-Hop Has the Microphone

After 25 years of shape-shifting development, hip-hop culture has not loosened its grip on youth, popular culture, or corporate America. The leaders of this industry continue to reinvent its marketing muscle, maintaining its influence and grasp on the global society.

Russell Simmons' Rush Communications had grown beyond its beginnings in music and fashion, via Def Jam and Phat Farm, and is now a presence in television (RSTV), talent management (SLBG), advertising (Rush Media), publishing (One World magazine), and film (Def Pictures). Simmons eventually founded a music publishing arm, named Rushtown Music, and a company for his philanthropy efforts, labeled Rush Arts.

In July 2001, two months before the United States suffered its most catastrophic terrorist attack, Simmons decided it was time to bring hip-hop into politics with hopes of getting urban youths involved in the shaping of our world. He helped to launch the creation of the Hip-Hop Summit Action Network (HSAN), a coalition of rap artists, record company executives, civil rights leaders, and community activists with the goal of galvanizing the hip-hop generation.

The nonprofit mobilization was inspired by a meeting held earlier in the year among record company executives, artists, and other key figures to discuss the state of hip-hop in terms of mass marketing and image.

In the June 2002 issue of leading hip-hop publication *Source*, Simmons and HSAN CEO Benjamin Chavis Muhammad wrote an essay titled "Power Movement," which outlined a 15-point agenda for the new group. Ranking number one was the "social, political and economic development and empowerment of our families and communities." Other key goals included an involvement in environmental issues and the push for reparations to address damages to blacks as a result of slavery.

Another major concern of Simmons and HSAN was the Federal Trade Commission's finding in 2001 that record companies continue to market albums with explicit lyrics to minors while other industries, such as advertising, film, and video games, have taken steps to curb such behavior. Sen. Joseph Lieberman, D-Conn., a harsh critic of the music industry, announced that he and other lawmakers would lean on the five biggest music companies with demands that they stop targeting inappropriate records to children.

With HSAN only four months old, Simmons decided the issue of government censorship would be the group's first major political battle. On October 1, 2002, Simmons and Chavis Muhammad visited Capitol Hill to testify on the subject before the Senate Subcommittee on Telecommunications and the Internet. "The Congress of the United States should not censor free speech nor artistic expression. It is unconstitutional for government intrusion or dictation concerning 'labeling of music' or 'rating of music' that has the effect of denying free speech," Simmons said in his prepared statement to the committee members.

Suggesting race played a factor in the federal crackdown on hip-hop lyrics, Simmons added: "The Federal Trade Commission's report on explicit content disproportionately focused on black hip-hop artists. These reports are flawed scientifically as well as morally and culturally and should not, therefore, be used as a basis for constructing a system of 'ratings' in regard to music and other forms of entertainment."

Soon, Simmons brought HSAN to the forefront of another issue that had emerged involving the soft drink company Pepsi and the cancellation of its commercial featuring rapper Ludacris.

After conservative television host Bill O'Reilly of Fox News Channel protested Pepsi's use of the Atlanta recording artist in its advertising campaign because of his raunchy lyrics, the company fired the rapper and hired in his place heavy metal icon Ozzy Osbourne, who some would argue is just as lyrically risqué as Ludacris.

Because Ludacris is a black hip-hop artist and Osbourne is a white rock legend, Simmons felt Pepsi's move smacked of a double standard. As a result, Simmons and HSAN organized a rally to call for a boycott of PepsiCo. "It had cultural overtones, cultural insensitivity," Simmons said of the company's decision to hire Osbourne, who at the time starred in his own profanity-filled MTV reality show, *The Osbournes*.

Before the boycott could take root, Pepsi admitted acting too hastily in the matter and agreed to donate about $3 million to youth charities involved in arts and music education, according to the *New York Times*. With the agreement, HSAN scored its first major victory as an organized political arm on behalf of hip-hop.

A strict vegetarian, Russell Simmons joined People for the Ethical Treatment of Animals (PETA) in a protest against KFC. He called for a boycott of the fast-food chain due to their unethical treatment of chickens. In the photograph above, Russell Simmons is honored with a 2001 PETA Humanitarian Award.

Moving further into politics, Simmons met with New York Governor George Pataki to discuss ways of modernizing the state's harsh Rockefeller drug laws, which at the time were the toughest mandatory-sentencing policies in the nation for drug offenders. In the 2006 documentary *Lockdown USA*, which chronicles Simmons' fight to repeal the Rockefeller laws, statistics regarding the offenders suggest a disproportionate number of African Americans are affected. According to the film, 93 percent of all those incarcerated from these laws are people of color. The film further states that even rapists receive lesser sentences than those sentenced under the Rockefeller drug laws.

Simmons' meeting with Pataki to repeal the laws stalled, and furthermore, Simmons wound up being sued by the Temporary State Commission for organizing a rally on the issue without registering first as a lobbyist. Outraged, Simmons filed a countersuit on grounds that his rally did not require registration as a lobbyist because he was simply exercising his freedom of speech as outlined by the U.S. Constitution. In August 2004, the court ruled that sections of the lobbying law were indeed unconstitutional because they allowed the state to fine lobbyists without giving them proper hearings. HSAN had scored another major victory in the political realm.

For Simmons, the importance of standing up for one's beliefs "on behalf of hip-hop," as he told one journalist, proved true for matters in his personal life as well. Just as he stood up to the state of New York, the die-hard yoga enthusiast and vegetarian soon turned his attention to the mistreatment and slaughter of animals. In August 2003, he joined People for the Ethical Treatment of Animals (PETA) in an all-out war against KFC.

Simmons called for a boycott of the fast-food chain for its practices of raising and slaughtering chickens. The mogul took out a full-page ad in the *Courier-Journal* in Louisville, Kentucky, where KFC is headquartered, and expressed his discontent in an open letter to David C. Novak, CEO of Yum Brands, which owns KFC. "What KFC does to 750 million chickens each

Russell Simmons is an advocate for healthy living, extolling the virtues of his vegetarian and yoga-practicing lifestyle. In 2005, he came out with the *Russell Simmons Presents Yoga Live* video series. In the photograph above, Russell Simmons is seen leaving a yoga studio in New York City with his two daughters.

year, on your watch, is not civilized or acceptable, and you can change that," the letter read. "I am calling for a boycott of all KFC restaurants until my friends at PETA tell me that you have agreed to be kinder in your practices."

Yum Brands released a statement claiming that KFC is not involved with the slaughter of chickens, only the buying, selling, and cooking of the animals. The health-conscious Simmons, however, was able to use the publicity surrounding the boycott to underscore his own promotion of wholesome living. Two years later, his company Simmons Lathan Media Group released the *Russell Simmons Presents Yoga Live* video series. A statement from SLMG President Will Griffin explained of the venture: "Our goal is always to bring our culture to the widest possible audience by partnering with the best in class distribution and marketing companies."

Publicizing his vegan diet and yoga practice, Simmons established himself as a symbol of healthy living and was able to market the benefits of his lifestyle to the hip-hop community. In 2004, the entertainment mogul and political figure found a way to profit from another aspect of his lavish lifestyle.

Simmons and his wife, Kimora, entered into a partnership with diamond distributor M. Fabrikant & Sons to launch The Simmons Jewelry Co. Under the deal, multiple jewelry lines would be created under the brands Baby Phat, Phat Farm, Def Jam, Kimora Lee Simmons, and Russell Simmons. The couple would join a team of merchandisers to design the jewelry, including a Red Carpet couture line featuring a signature-cut diamond. "Teaming up and partnering with a company as solid and as reputable as Fabrikant on this venture will hopefully influence other African Americans to actively participate in businesses that they influence around the world," the couple said in a statement.

In addition to inspiring African Americans to engage in business opportunities, it was also important for Simmons that urban youths take command of their financial future and

In July 2006, Russell Simmons was named a United Nations Goodwill Ambassador for his efforts to educate and empower young people using hip-hop music and culture. In the photograph above, Simmons speaks at the New York City model UN conference at the United Nations Headquarters.

take steps to remove debt. In 2005, he created two such entities: UniRush Financial Services, which partnered with Intuit's
TurboTax to help 18- to 24-year-olds file their income taxes,
and the prepaid debit Rush Card, targeted to the roughly 70
million people who are without a banking account.

While Simmons made sure he remained at the forefront of
emerging financial opportunities for the hip-hop generation,
his various other ventures were also making strides. In 2005,
Simmons's SLMG teamed with Sean "Diddy" Combs's Bad Boy

SPIRULINA

Spirulina offers remarkable health benefits to undernourished
people. It is rich in beta-carotene that can overcome eye problems caused by Vitamin A deficiency. The protein and B-vitamin
complex makes a major nutritional improvement in an infant's
diet. It is the only food source, except for mother's milk, contain-
ing substantial amounts of an essential fatty acid, GLA, that helps
regulate the entire hormone system.

One tablespoon a day can eliminate iron anemia, the most
common mineral deficiency. Spirulina is the most digestible protein food, especially important for malnourished people whose
intestines can no longer absorb nutrients effectively. These health
benefits have made it an excellent food for rapid recovery of children with malnutrition related diseases in many countries.

CISRI-ISP is recognized as the permanent observer mission
with the United Nations Economic and Social Council. CISRI-ISP
maintains communication with the United Nations World Food
and Agriculture Organization, World Health Organization, and the
World Food Programme.

TV to produce *Run's House,* a reality show for MTV centered on his brother Reverend Run and his family. The show continues to be one of the highest rated programs on the music channel.

In 2006, SLMG signed a multiyear development deal with HBO to produce scripted series, specials, and other projects—the first being a comedy series called *The Unsuccessful Thug,* starring comedian Mike Epps. Additionally, the partnership fostered the return of *Russell Simmons' Def Comedy Jam* in September, with Epps as host.

The year 2006 also brought along two distinct honors that placed Russell Simmons among society's elite and reaffirmed his position as a leader in social and political justice. In February, the city of Newark, New Jersey, awarded Simmons a key to the city in honor of his work with the Hip-Hop Summit Action Network, and in July, he became a United Nations Goodwill Ambassador for his efforts in using hip-hop to educate youth about world issues.

With the title of Permanent Observer Missionary for Collaborative Intergovernmental Scientific Research Institute-Intergovernmental Spirulina Program (CISRI-ISP), an intergovernmental organization that fights hunger and malnutrition around the world, Simmons is tasked with helping to educate young people about the issue. "We're going to help save lives. We will not be silenced in the face of the awful fact that more than 40,000 people die every day from malnutrition and poverty. That is unacceptable to the hip-hop community," Simmons said in a statement.

The United Nations title is certainly a crowning achievement for Russell Simmons, who took his love of hip-hop and made it into a multimillion-dollar business that expanded beyond its musical borders into fashion, television, film, advertising, publishing, lifestyle, jewelry, politics, health, and philanthropy.

DISCOGRAPHY

ALBUMS (PRODUCER)

Radio, LL Cool J.1985.

Oran "Juice" Jones, Oran "Juice" Jones.1986.

License to Ill, Beastie Boys.1986.

Reign In Blood, Slayer.1986.

Yo! Bum Rush the Show, Public Enemy.1987.

Bigger and Deffer, LL Cool J.1987.

Fear of a Black Planet, Public Enemy.1990.

Mama Said Knock You Out, LL Cool J.1990.

Apocalype 91: The Enemy Strikes Black, Public Enemy.1991.

The Ruler is Back, Slick Rick.1991.

Greatest Misses, Public Enemy.1992.

Whut Thee Album, Redman. 1992.

14 Shots to the Dome, LL Cool J. 1993.

Mr. Smith, LL Cool J. 1994.

1957   Russell Simmons is born on October 4 to Evelyn and
Daniel Simmons in New York City.

1965   The Simmons family moves to Hollis, a community
in the southeast section of Queens, New York.

1975   Russell attends City College in the Harlem area of
New York.

1979   Under manager Russell Simmons, Kurtis Blow
becomes the first rapper to sign a recording deal
with a major record company. His first single is
"Christmas Rappin'."

1984   Russell Simmons meets a college student named Rick
Rubin, an avid fan of rap music. Simmons and Rubin
form a business partnership, which creates Def Jam
Records. The business operates out of Rubin's college
dorm room at NYU.

1984   The *Wall Street Journal* declares Russell Rap
Music's Mogul.

1985   Def Jam releases its first album, 16-year-old LL Cool J's
debut, *Radio*.

1985   Def Jam finances and releases rap movie *Krush
Groove*. The film is based on Russell Simmons's life.
Actor Blair Underwood plays Russell; Run-DMC,
Kurtis Blow, the Fat Boys, and the newly signed
Beastie Boys have roles in the film.

1986   Hip-hop's first white rap group, the Beastie Boys,
release their debut album, *Licensed to Ill*, on Def Jam
Records. It goes on to become the best-selling rap
album of the decade.

1988   Rick Rubin leaves Def Jam and forms a new label,
Def American.

1988 Public Enemy releases its second album, *It Takes A Nation of Millions to Hold Us Back*. With its use of dense, layered sampling, hard funk, and politically incendiary rhymes, it is hailed by rap and rock critics alike as a landmark recording. Public Enemy skyrockets toward the forefront of popular music.

1989 2Live Crew releases its album *As Nasty as They Wanna Be*. The lyrics are extremely explicit and the album is banned from sale in the group's home state of Florida. The group members themselves are arrested for lewdness; a heated debate over the First Amendment develops.

1992 Simmons invests $500,000 to start the Phat Farm clothing line.

1994 Simmons develops *Def Comedy Jam* for HBO, inspired by The Comedy Act Theatre in Los Angeles.

1998 Simmons marries Kimora Lee on December 20, 1998; his brother Rev Run presides over the ceremony.

1998 Russell Simmons, Sean "Puff Daddy" Combs, and Master P all appear in *Forbes* magazine as the Top Moneymakers in Entertainment.

2000 Universal Music Group purchases half of Simmons share in Def Jam Records for more than $100 million.

2001 Simmons launches Hip-Hop Summit Action Network, dedicated to harnessing the cultural relevance of hip-hop music to serve as a catalyst for education advocacy and to empower youth.

2001 *Def Poetry Jam*, hosted by Mos Def, debuts on HBO.

2003   Hip-Hop Summit Action Network launches Hip-Hop Team Vote, a voter-registration initiative.

2004   Simmons, Kimora Lee Simmons, and the Rush Philanthropic Arts Foundation, in partnership with the Art for Life Palm Beach benefit gala, raise $600,000 for disadvantaged youths in New York City and Palm Beach, Florida.

2005   Hip-Hop Summit Action Network begins a six-city "Get Your Money Right" tour to teach methods to stay out of debt and gain financial success.

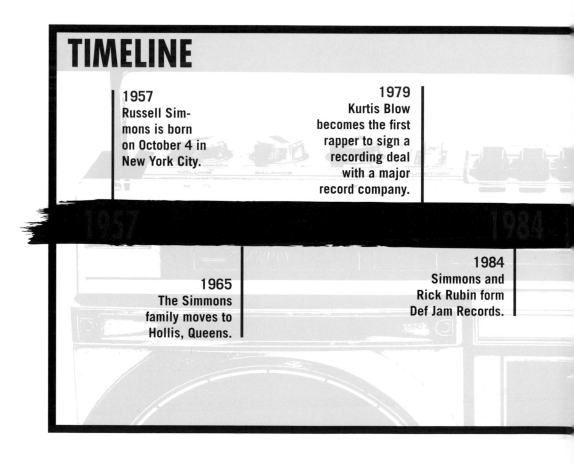

TIMELINE

1957
Russell Simmons is born on October 4 in New York City.

1979
Kurtis Blow becomes the first rapper to sign a recording deal with a major record company.

1965
The Simmons family moves to Hollis, Queens.

1984
Simmons and Rick Rubin form Def Jam Records.

2006 Simmons initiates the Diamond Empowerment Fund to teach Africans how to cut and polish diamonds rather than simply mining them.

Russell and Kimora Lee Simmons announce separation.

2007 Simmons's book *Do You! 12 Laws to Access the Power in You to Achieve Happiness and Success* is published.

Simmons and HSAN issue a statement urging rappers and the recording industry to remove or "bleep" certain offensive words from song lyrics.

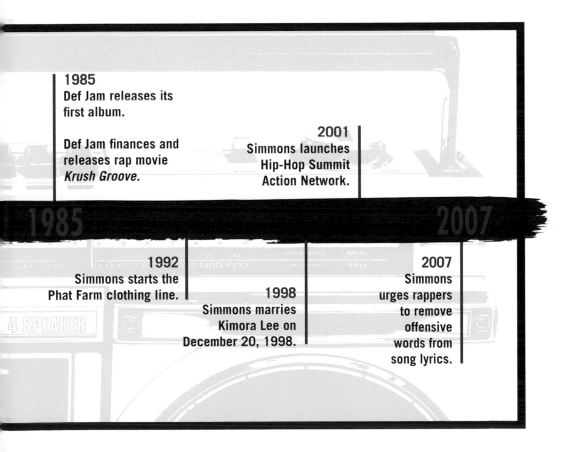

1985
Def Jam releases its first album.

Def Jam finances and releases rap movie *Krush Groove.*

2001
Simmons launches Hip-Hop Summit Action Network.

1985   2007

1992
Simmons starts the Phat Farm clothing line.

1998
Simmons marries Kimora Lee on December 20, 1998.

2007
Simmons urges rappers to remove offensive words from song lyrics.

4 SPEAKER

freestyling   To ad-lib vocally. This process is both a skill and an art form. Freestyling is popular among MCs in the hip-hop scene.

hip-hop   A popular urban youth culture, closely associated with rap music and with the style and fashions of African-American inner-city residents.

MC   A master of ceremonies or MC (sometimes spelled emcee) is the host of a staged event or other performance. The MC usually presents performers, speaks to the audience, and generally keeps the show moving.

phat   To be very good, especially in reference to music and viewable content. Something of high quality.

rap   The rhythmic delivery of rhymes over a beat or a cappella. Rap occupies a gray area between speech, poetry, and song.

sampling   The act of taking a portion of one sound recording, the sample, and reusing it as an instrument or element of a new recording.

scratching   Moving a vinyl record back and forth with the hand while it is playing on a turntable. This creates a distinctive sound that became one of the most recognizable features of hip-hop music.

turntabling   Using recorded notes and sounds from other instruments to allow a DJ to mimic the sounds of an musical instrument. This allows a DJ to make traditional sounding music by using a digital turntable instead of playing an instrument.

▸ ▸▸ BIBLIOGRAPHY ▪ ‖

Alim, H. Samy. "Hip Hop Nation Language." In *Language in the USA*. Edward Finegan, and John Rickford, editors. New York: Cambridge University Press, 2004.

Appleson, Gail. "Nelly Will Host Summit Here to Rap About Dollars and Sense." *St. Louis Post–Dispatch,* August 18, 2005.

Chuck D. *Fight the Power: Rap, Race, and Reality*. New York: Delacorte Press, 1997.

Dingle, Derek T. *Black Enterprise: Titans of the B.E. 100*. New York: John Wiley & Sons, 1999.

Forman, Murray. *The 'hood: Race, Space and Place in Rap and Hip hop*. Middletown, Conn.: Wesleyan Press. 2002.

Gueraseva, Stacy. *Def Jam, Inc: Russell Simmons, Rick Rubin, and the Extraordinary Story of the World's Most Influential Hip-Hop Label*. New York: Ballantine Books, 2005.

Liles, Kevin. *Make It Happen: The Hip-Hop Generation Guide to Success*. New York: Atria, 2005.

Simmons, Russell. *Life and Def: Sex, Drugs, Money + God*. New York: Crown Publishers, 2001.

Sisario, Ben. "Hip Hop Finds a Home at the Smithsonian," *New York Times*, March 5, 2006.

Webber, Stephen. *TurntableTechnique: The Art of the D.J.* Boston: Berklee Press Publications, 2000.

Green, Jared. *Examining Pop Culture: Rap and Hip Hop.* Chicago: Greenhaven Press, 2003.

Greene, Meg. *Lauryn Hill.* New York: Chelsea House Publishers, 2000.

Gueraseva, Stacy. *Def Jam, Inc.: Russell Simmons, Rick Rubin, and the Extraordinary Story of the World's Most Influential Hip-Hop Label.* New York: Ballantine Books, 2005.

Hagar, Steven. *Hip Hop; The Illustrated History of Break Dancing, Rap Music, and Graffiti.* New York: St. Martin's Press, 1984.

Hebdige, Dick. *Cut 'N' Mix; Culture, Identity and Caribbean Music.* New York: Methuen, 1987.

Jones, Maurice K. *Say It Loud: The Story of Rap Music.* Brookfield, Conn.: Millbrook Press, 1994.

Stauffer, Stacy. *Will Smith.* New York: Chelsea House Publishers, 1999.

Toop, David. *The Rap Attack; African Jive to New York Hip Hop.* Boston: South End Press, 1984.

WEB SITES

www.Aerosmith.com

http://allhiphop.com

www.Rushphilanthropic.org

www.youthspecialties.com

▸ ▸▸ PHOTO CREDITS ▪ ‖

PAGE

COVER

Getty Images North America/Getty Images

▶ ▸▸ INDEX ■ ॥

Index

▸ ▸ **ABOUT THE AUTHORS** ■ ‖

COOKIE LOMMEL started her career as a journalist in the entertainment industry. She has served as entertainment editor for *Teen* magazine, associate editor for *Radio & Records* magazine, and editor at large for *Black Elegance* magazine. Lommel has interviewed hundreds of film, television, and music personalities as an on-camera reporter for CNN and has written numerous biographies for young adults.

CHUCK D redefined rap music and hip-hop culture as leader and cofounder of legendary rap group Public Enemy. His messages addressed weighty issues about race, rage, and inequality with a jolting combination of intelligence and eloquence. A musician, writer, radio host, TV guest, college lecturer, and activist, he is the creator of Rapstation.com, a multiformat home on the Web for the vast global hip-hop community.

YA
B
SIMMONS
LO

MAIN LIBRARY

Lommel, Cookie.

Russell Simmons.

Wallingford Public Library
Wallingford, CT 06492

A2170 559708 1

MAIN LIBRARY

WALLINGFORD PUBLIC LIBRARY
200 NO MAIN ST
WALLINGFORD CT 06492

BAKER & TAYLOR